Aging, Ailments, and Attitudes

by

Cathy Lee Phillips

Sara,
Enjoy the precious
gift of each new
day.
Cathy Lee Phillips

Patchwork Press, Ltd.
P. O. Box 4684
Canton, Georgia 30115
www.patchworkpress.com

Aging, Ailments, and Attitudes

Library of Congress Control Number:
2003096063

Published by:
Patchwork Press, Ltd.
P. O. Box 4684
Canton, Georgia 30115
www.patchworkpress.com

ISBN 0-9715925-3-5

Printed in the United States by Morris Publishing
3212 East Highway 30 • Kearney, NE 68847
1-800-650-7888

Other Books by Cathy Lee Phillips

🐝 *Silver in the Slop and Other Surprises*

🐝 *Gutsy Little Flowers*

🐝 *Silver Reflections: A Daily Journal*

Order from:

Patchwork Press, Ltd.
P. O. Box 4684
Canton, Georgia 30115
770-720-7988
www.patchworkpress.com

Dedicated To

Deborah Jackson Mason

When I visited a Sunday School class at Chamblee United Methodist Church a few years ago, I had no idea I would meet a new best friend, confidante, and sister. How ironic that we grew up in the same hometown, yet had to come to Chamblee to meet. How amazingly similar our lives were during our Newnan years. I wish we had known one another then and could have shared our parallel pains and triumphs. But you are here now and what a blessing you are! The pains and triumphs will continue, no doubt, but I thank God for the gift of a sister with whom I can share my laughter, tears, and deepest thoughts. You hold a very special place in my life, Deborah, one I know will continue right through our "golden girl" years and beyond.

Thank you for so many things – for long conversations, for an unforgettable 40th birthday party, for "broo-ty pageants" and my "Her Serene Highness O Published One" Crown, for our Ritz adventures, for being the best kitchen and pantry organizer on the planet, for traveling with me and laughing at the bra story even though you have heard it a gazillion times, for envisioning the book trilogy, and for talking me through my meltdowns as well as celebrating my moments that seem downright miraculous. Thank you for wanting me to succeed so much that you put your best efforts into helping me achieve my goals (You are the best Project Manager Patchwork Press has ever had!). Thank you for showing me the unconditional love a parent should have for a child. You have raised Drew with wisdom and patience and have every reason to be proud of the young man he is becoming.

Despite these things, you do have your flaws. You still haven't learned to drive faster than 35 MPH and you dress in fleece and long underwear during the summer. Other than that, you're just about perfect . . . which really gets on my nerves! But I love you – and Drew – and I thank God for blessing my life with both of you.

--Cathy

Table of Contents

Foreword

By Wednesday's Girls

We've decided that since we're all aging (gracefully, of course), have a few ailments (none too serious but typically caused by falling down stairs, or by falling over each other laughing), and certainly possess Attitude (with a capital A), we should have a few things to say about Cathy Lee Phillips and this new book of hers.

But first, let's have some snacks.

Go get yourself one of our favorites: a giant-sized cup of Diet Coke, a mug of coffee, or a bottle of water, and while you're at it, fix yourself some muffins. We'll invite you to join our Disciple Bible study group for a few moments. You can be one of "Wednesday's Girls." And, if you're a man, well, work with us here.

It was a Wednesday, a typical late-summer day in Georgia – hot and getting hotter, that is – when we first met Cathy. We gathered around a dining room table, passed the fruit salad and cranberry coffee cake, opened Bibles, and started to get acquainted.

Cathy, who was to be the de facto leader of our study for the next 32 weeks, asked us to go through the typical preliminaries of a small group that was meeting for the first time: tell your name and a little bit about yourself, and share your favorite Bible verse.

By the time the seven of us were done that morning, we had filled out our prayer list for the week and lined up the snack rotation for the upcoming months. We knew a little bit more about each other, and we were left with a prevailing thought from St. Francis of Assisi – shared by Cathy – to propel us forward together:

> *"Always be a witness for Christ;*
> *if necessary, use words."*

We dutifully scribbled down the phrase that day, but in the following eight months that quote became etched on our hearts and minds. Together, we sorrowed at the illness and death of a mother, rejoiced at the birth of a healthy baby, shared fears of the future, noted the trials and triumphs of life, and celebrated God's grace. We spent hours talking about other relatives and friends who were facing times of trial, and how they – and we – responded to such difficulty.

> *"Always be a witness for Christ;*
> *if necessary, use words."*

We discovered in those many months that Cathy Lee Phillips uses words when necessary, in book form and through retreats and speaking engagements, to be a witness for Christ. But behind those words first is a life lived with passion, love, humility, dedication, and faith.

Each week we'd look for her Grand "Viagra" SUV (aka Suzuki Grand Vitara) – as her other friends call it – to come careening down the road. Though she lived nearly 45 minutes away, she remained committed to us and to our weekly study, and she added measurably to our discussions. Cathy gives to others more gifts than can be named, including kindness, love, and laughter. She has the unique ability to see clearly life situations that the rest of us might miss, and sees these situations with a loving but humorous flair.

Our time together as Wednesday's Girls gave us spiritual nourishment for each week as well as precious friendships grounded in Christ. Girlfriends, we know, are a major part of coping with aging, whether we're celebrating a rite of passage together or ranting at the inevitability of it all.

When you read Cathy's writing you have a sense that she is telling the story while sitting with you, and you become better in some way . . . your spirit is lifted, you are encouraged to be what God intended, or you smile or laugh at the hilarious story that has just been told. Cathy's writing is a gift to us in that we are able to continue our Wednesday morning fellowship . . . all that is needed is a good snack, beverage of choice, and Cathy's guidance and sense of humor.

We invite you to be a part of this fellowship – just grab your snack and turn the page!

Wednesday's Girls
July 2003

Debbie Guest
Amy Hoogervorst
Michelle Salle
Dawn Troke
Beth Whitson
Lisa Wills

Acknowledgements

A few weeks ago I had a dream come true – I was Cinderella for a day! Bonnie Johnson and her cohorts at Lewis Memorial United Methodist Church (Augusta, Georgia) invited me to present a program for the women of their church and community. I began the day as "Lucinda Poteet," a crude, friendless, talkative hag. What a stretch for me!

Minutes later I was transformed into Cinderella – the lonely stepchild whose Fairy Godmother made it possible for her to go to the ball and marry her Prince Charming. As Cinderella, I wore a sparkling gown with a flowing train, a design straight from the sewing room of my friend, Mimi Smith. A borrowed tiara, rhinestone jewels, and about ten pounds of stage makeup completed the ensemble.

I was a princess, even if only for a few hours. Ultimately, I traded my gown for a pair of shorts and returned the tiara to its rightful owner. And my Prince Charming (who, in my mind, looks like Dylan McDermott) never appeared to whisk me off to "happily ever after."

It was just a program for a group of women. But, whatever the explanation, I was a princess for a little while.

Even though there is currently no tiara or Prince Charming in the picture, I do seem to have an abundance of Fairy Godmothers – friends and colleagues who love me enough to pray, guide, and assist me in accomplishing my goals and dreams. No one lives or works completely alone and I am blessed with an abundance of people who have helped me reach my dream of being a fulltime writer, speaker, and singer – as well as the goal of completing this book. Every one of you, named and unnamed, has my deepest love and gratitude.

Just over a year ago I received a call from a woman who introduced herself as Stacy Robinson, President of the Robinson Agency.

"May I represent you?" she asked after we talked for a while.

Saying yes to this incredible opportunity was a no-brainer! Stacy has provided opportunities for ministry as well as practical advice on improving my work. The ultimate professional, Stacy conducts her business in a genuine Christian manner. I am honored to be a part of The Robinson Agency. Thanks, Stacy!

Last year Stacy arranged for me to appear on *Babbie's House*, a weekly TV show hosted by Dove award-winning singer, songwriter, recording artist, and author, Babbie Mason. A few weeks later, Babbie called to request permission to feature my story, *Silver in the Slop*, in her latest book, *Faith Lift*. I was happy to grant permission. Babbie has kindly provided a beautiful endorsement for this book. I am astonishment by Babbie's incredible talent and faith. I am even more astonished that I can call her *friend*.

A big hug goes to each of Wednesday's Girls, an incredible group of Christian women. We became a family as we met each week for a nine-month Disciple Bible study. From birth to death, we covered every topic imaginable. These friends are dear to me and their writing the Foreword for this book is one of the most precious gifts I have ever received.

Mrs. Earlene Scott, owner of Scott's Bookstore in my hometown of Newnan, Georgia, will always and forever host all my inaugural book-signings. Mrs. Earlene and her staff are unsurpassed and I enjoy every moment I spend with them. Speaking of Newnan, I am enjoying a new friendship with Angela Webster – a talented writer who will eventually write her own books. If not, I will have to hurt her!

A few years ago, Alice Smith, Editor of the *Wesleyan Christian Advocate* (the Official News Source of Georgia Methodism), invited me to write a regular column for this award-winning publication. It has been a pleasure to work with Alice and the staff of the Advocate. It has also been a pleasure to receive e-mail and letters of support from readers who have enjoyed my columns.

I enjoyed two beautiful writing retreats while completing this book. Margie Franklin offered her cozy mountain cabin while Barbara and Roy Olson provided their lovely home on Lake Lanier. And when I needed new promotional material, Rob and Michelle Thilenius came to the rescue with their creativity and eye for detail. These guys are the best across-the-street neighbors anyone could have. Meanwhile, Jim Turner and Kristin Luther handle business details that drive me crazy. Perhaps that is why I have not been very good at getting information to them quicker.

The Patchwork Press website exists due to the work of Caroline Sosebee, Webmaster Extraordinaire. She deciphers my notes and e-mails, which then magically appear on my web page. I wish I possessed her computer wisdom.

And when it comes to help, I simply must mention Stacy Strickland Benton – a great organizer and the Grand Poo-Bah of Personal Assistants.

My writing has provided the opportunity to reconnect with former teachers including Virginia Cox, Janie Lore, Sarah Estes, Dr. Frank McCook, and many others. When they say, "I'm proud of you," it is a priceless gift.

My deepest gratitude goes to Mary, Phil, Kaden, Katie, Joey, Debbie & Bill, Fred & Martha, Jane & Warren, Sue Lynn, Connie, Gene & Mimi, Norma, Claudia, Jamie, Jennifer, Betty Wallace, Dee the Troll of Trolls, and Lauren, for reasons they will understand. A big thanks goes to the Pre-DM Jones Chapel Gang who will always be family to me. As always, Neil keeps me grounded with his humor and insights.

There are certain groups to whom I am thankful. Many friends have graciously allowed me to use their names and stories. Some, in fact, call me when they stumble across something they believe will make a great story. Usually they are right!

Finally, one group receives special recognition – those who have invited me into their churches, schools, civic clubs, and other organizations, to share my words and my books. I never expected to be a professional speaker, but you have made it easy. You have laughed and cried right along with me and offered me your friendship and support. Thank you for the opportunities to speak at Sunday worship services, Wednesday night dinners, Mother-Daughter Banquets, Christmas Banquets, Women's Events, Senior Adult Programs, etc. I have led more retreats than I can number and each has provided the opportunity to get to know new friends on a genuine level. So, here's to the Retreat Ladies who love me, teach me, support me, keep in touch with me, and even pay me for what I enjoy doing.

Oh, and a special salute goes to the Ha Ga Sisterhood – just because I love you!

And to Deborah – sister, friend, confidante – your friendship has been a wonderful blessing, except when you are driving, complaining about the temperature, or acting as Nurse Helga. As far as I am concerned, Alan is not the only star in the family – you are one in your own right!

Finally, I thank God for his wisdom, guidance, and unconditional love. God has provided more strength than I could have envisioned and has remained constant when everything else in my life seemed to be fading away. God will be the one unwavering support that guides me through this process of aging and, ultimately, leads me into eternity.

When speaking to different groups, I often ask, "Do you know how to make God chuckle?"

The answer? "Tell him your plans."

For years I told God my plans and asked him to jump on board and make them happen. I had my own visions of how I would become Cinderella and make it to the palace. I simply wanted God to make my plans a reality. Well, it has taken quite a few years, but I have finally learned to discern the plan God has for me. Some days I fail, but other days I hit the mark. My faith is renewed every day and enables me to travel roads I would never have imagined when I was telling God what to do. But that was when I told God my plans.

Well, things are different now. I am wiser and I know that it is God who should make the plans for my life and future.

That, my friends, is wisdom that only comes from aging!

--*Cathy Lee Phillips*
Canton, Georgia
August 2003

A new broom sweeps clean,
but an old one knows the corners.

--English Saying

☒☒☒☒☒☒☒

The older I get,
the greater power I seem to have to help the world;
I am like a snowball –
the further I am rolled, the more I gain.

--Susan B. Anthony
(1820-1906)

1

Cathy Lee Phillips

Overview

Wrinkles
should merely indicate
where the
smiles have been.

--Mark Twain
(1835-1910)

3

Today
I bent over
to tie my shoe . . .

. . . and my
neck
and
stomach
got into a fight
with each other.

So This Is Aging?

*A*s I write these words, I am forty-six years old. 46! I have no problem sharing my age and have never understood why many keep theirs hidden. There are those who lie about their age altogether, while others keep it as classified as NORAD defense codes, the Colonel's original chicken recipe, or the Classic Coke formula.

Why is that? Consider the alternative. Aging is a privilege that, regretfully, is denied to some. I have learned a great deal during these forty-six years and am proud to still be around to share some of the lessons. I never thought I would live to be forty-six. It wasn't so long ago that I believed thirty was practically prehistoric and anyone that old undoubtedly grew up in a cave with a pet dinosaur instead of a family dog. Well, I am no longer thirty; in fact, I passed that birthday some sixteen years ago and, I assure you, I've never owned a dinosaur in my life.

Despite my frank attitude about aging, I will admit that I am more than thrilled when people say, "Why, you certainly don't look forty-six!" or "You act and look so young – I would never have known you were in your forties."

Of course, when you are seventeen, it is an insult to be told that you look young. These days, however, it is quite nice to hear! And long ago I promised myself that, though I might be getting older, I am never going to be OLD. Sounds good, huh? This is a positive mindset but one that doesn't so easily hold true when your joints are aching and you reach for your bifocals the first thing each morning.

Consequently, I have developed a means of explaining some of the inconvenient issues associated with this process called aging. Some may say I am rationalizing. Some may say I am not really in touch with the issues at hand. Nevertheless, these observations are merely my means of explaining what is now happening to my mind and body.

Read on, my friend. No doubt, you have faced some of these same concerns and can appreciate my thoughts. Feel free to share my experience with others because, together, we can learn as we grow older . . . but never OLD!

⧖⧖⧖⧖⧖⧖⧖

Regarding Hair . . .

Aging can be summed up in a nutshell and it is all about hair. Briefly – men want it on their heads and women do not want it on their faces. That is the basic rule, but there are other issues regarding hair that are pertinent to our discussion.

For instance, I have noticed that quite a few of my friends have been plagued with the aggravation of gray hair. Some have sprouted just a small amount while others are literally consumed with the cursed stuff. Many believe gray hair to be a sign of wisdom and, while I want to be wise, I just don't want to be too wise too soon.

Therefore I am pleased that this sure sign of aging has not yet afflicted me.

I have noticed, though, that I do have a few strands of hair – only two or three at the most – that are of a lighter hue than the remainder of my hair. While it is understandable that some might consider these strands to be gray, they would be woefully mistaken. I have seen many men and women with beautiful gray hair. However, I want to clearly state that my hair is certainly not gray. In fact, there is a simple explanation – these particular strands are anemic.

Because of my hectic schedule, extensive travel, and intense stress, I have obviously developed a mild case of anemia that has, yea verily, affected the very hair on my head. This particular form of anemia inhibits the blood flow to my head (yes, I am aware that many people will readily agree with this diagnosis). However, I am not talking about blood flow to the brain; I am talking about blood flow to the hair follicles.

Upon reflection, I believe that this ailment began several years ago following my third knee operation. Obviously, the anesthesia administered during surgery is quite powerful – forceful enough to place the body into an overpowering slumber. Thankfully, I awakened following surgery. However, it seems obvious that not all of my hair follicles awakened with me. I am convinced, therefore, that the anesthesia used in this surgical procedure obviously contained hair-anemia producing tendencies. Why else would I have suddenly noticed pale strands amid my chestnut hair so quickly after surgery?

I understand how pale hair might be easily confused with gray hair. Yet, they are vastly different. Gray hair is a sign of the aging process and makes one look and feel older until Miss Clairol enters the picture.

On the other hand, pale is not a color. A pale hair is simply one that is lighter than the others on my head and, undoubtedly, is caused by *medically-induced hair anemia.*

Have you undergone a medical procedure lately? Think about it. The hair that has been pestering you may not be gray at all. Like me, you may simply be experiencing the unwelcome presence of anemic hair.

Rest assured that under these conditions, it is perfectly acceptable to invite Miss Clairol into your home or to visit your local hair salon to restore your pale strands to their original color. You are tackling a medical condition and, as such, I believe it should be quite acceptable to file all hair color expenses with your health insurance carrier.

Meanwhile, you may want to consider adjusting your diet. My research indicates that robust amounts of red meat, chocolate, and various flavors of cheesecake, may actually reverse *medically-induced hair anemia.* Of course, these dietary changes may cause cholesterol levels to rise. But we all know that looking good is far more important than some silly little cholesterol number!

⏳⏳⏳⏳⏳⏳⏳

Regarding Eyes . . .

As aging occurs, certain individuals develop irritating wrinkles – fine lines – around the eyes. Though I know nothing about them personally, I have seen them on the faces of others.

Your eyes are wonderful communicators. They twinkle when you experience happiness and fill with tears when times are painful. In addition, your eyes (and the rest of your face) are exposed to the extremes of hot and cold weather throughout the years. Allergies cause dry, itchy eyes. And it is only natural to rub your eyes when they are strained from viewing computer screens, televisions, good books, and a million other things.

In other words, your eyes are prime targets for wrinkles.

While I am thankful I have not yet experienced the heartbreak of under-eye wrinkles, I am concerned about an incident that occurred a few weeks ago when I visited the mall.

I was strolling through a large department store minding my own business when a representative at the Lancôme counter grabbed me by the collar and wrestled me onto the glass display. When I regained consciousness, the woman was mopping the area under my eyes with a cool, soothing cream.

"What are you doing?" I cried, feeling like a quarterback who had just been sacked by an entire opposing team.

"Well, ma'am," she cheerfully spoke, "we now have cream to hide unsightly under-eye wrinkles."

When I realized she was talking to me, I was incensed! I was outraged! I was interested!

"Hey," I announced to her, "These are fine lines! Haven't you heard that term? I do not have wrinkles, although I may admit that due to allergies, fatigue, and overwork, I may have one or two barely visible fine lines."

I further informed this woman that, by the very nature of the term, it is fine to have these lines – they decorate your face and give it character.

Even though I obviously possessed no unsightly under-eye wrinkles, I was interested because this woman was exercising aggressive marketing, the hallmark of a successful business. Having my own business, I understand the importance of believing in your product and marketing it aggressively. I do that myself because selling my books helps others and keeps a roof over my head.

Likewise, this Lancôme representative obviously believed in her product and wanted me to try it just in case, one day in the distant future, I might need a cream for wrinkles around the eye. I also imagined that this woman worked on commission and needed to keep a roof over her own head. Maybe she was a single mother with twelve children and no other source of income because her ex-husband was jailed for non-payment of child support. Surely her children needed typical things such as braces, cheerleading uniforms, and college tuition. Perhaps she also had a nice dog that needed expensive heartworm medication. In short, this woman was most likely financially strapped which caused her to display this gruff, albeit completely understandable, behavior.

Aggressive marketing. Taking care of her children and a beloved pet. That is why this woman wrestled me to the counter. Who can blame her? In fact, I admire her. So I am sure you understand that my actually purchasing the product had nothing to do with my fear of wrinkles or fine lines. On the contrary, it was an act of Christian charity – one that would assist this fine aggressive marketer and dedicated mother. It was the least I could do.

That's all. No wrinkles here.

☒☒☒☒☒☒☒

Regarding Eyeglasses...

Visiting my ophthalmologist each year is one of my more enjoyable doctor visits. First of all, he is one seriously handsome fellow. Secondly, no stirrups are involved. During my most recent visit, my eye doctor happily explained the result of my exam.

"I have great news for you, Cathy," he explained. "You have no disease of the eye. All the things you are experiencing are typical symptoms of the aging process."

"And . . .?" I questioned.

"What else do you want to know?" my doctor asked.

"Well, I'm waiting for that good news you mentioned."

The Aging Process? I suppose that is preferable to having a disease of the eye, but who wants to be reminded that the aging process is dogging you?

My doctor did prescribe reading glasses. Of course, this is quite understandable. I spend my life reading, writing, and pounding a computer until late into the night. Eyestrain is a logical consequence of writing books. In fact, I believe my eye problems are related more to eyestrain than to any old aging process. My eyes obviously become fatigued because of extensive use.

For that reason, I have no problem with needing glasses. In fact, I wore glasses in college. And now they are even more in vogue with thousands of designer frames that are quite attractive. . . perchance, even sexy? Simply placing them on my face changes my look and personality. As a writer, I believe that a proper pair of glasses enhances the serious, scholarly image I wish to project. Think of John Boy Walton. Once he properly positioned his horn-rimmed glasses, he looked like an author with an extra degree of creativity, professionalism, and authority.

I wanted that look. Glasses would be good. But I was totally unprepared for the words my attractive doctor spoke next.

"Cathy, because you are a public speaker, I think it might be best if you get . . . bifocals."

"Bifocals?" I shrieked. "The 'B' word! You have just killed me. I cannot believe you used that word in my presence!"

Bifocals? Yes, I wanted the scholarly, professional look, but I did not want that look to include bifocals. The mere mention of that word evoked visions of thick coke-bottle lenses covered with lines and indentions placed inside ugly, black, gloomy frames. Bifocals are not the look of professionalism and authority. Bifocals are just the look of old eyes.

"Hear me out," he said quietly, and explained that as a public speaker, it would be best for me to have the "B" word glasses. When I read passages from my books, I put my glasses on. Then, when I look into the audience, I feel seasick because everything in the distance looks blurry, causing my stomach to flip-flop as if I had motion sickness. I then remove my glasses to calm my queasy stomach. My doctor wisely pointed out that taking my glasses off and on is very distracting to an audience. And because I have good distance vision, the upper part of my bifocals would simply be clear glass.

"So let me get this straight," speaking slowly to ensure I understood him correctly. "Based on what you have said, I do not actually need the 'B' word. You are suggesting this simply because of my profession and my effectiveness as a speaker."

I continued, "In fact, these glasses technically do not even meet the definition of bifocals because the upper part will merely be clear glass."

"Correct," my doctor assured me.

"So we really do not even need to use that 'B' word again when discussing my eyes," I confirmed.

Stifling a chuckle, my doctor agreed never again to use the "B" word in my presence.

Leaving his office, I drove to the one-hour vision shop at the mall. I presented my information to the sales representative, all the while explaining that despite the prescription, I did not really need bifocals. I explained my work, why I needed these particular spectacles, and why these glasses did not meet the criteria of true bifocals. I explained far more than the sales representative wanted to know.

Perhaps to stop my babbling, the sales rep pointed me toward their vast collection of frames. Choosing frames is a monumental task because they will convey your sense of style and elegance. The shape should compliment your face while highlighting the colors of your hair, eyes, and skin. In other words, this process cannot be rushed. The sales rep selected a pair of frames that I really liked but, of course, I had to look for myself. About ninety minutes and hundreds of frames later, I ultimately chose the frames the sales rep suggested – the very first pair I tried.

"These fit your face perfectly," he said excitedly, probably because I had finally made a decision. "Plus, they are just perfect for someone needing progressive lenses."

"Excuse me?" I questioned. "What did you say? Progressive lenses?"

"Yes, progressive lenses. Of course, I realize that these glasses technically do not fit the true definition of bifocals," he said with a smirk. "But in case you ever need them, be sure to ask for Progressive Lenses. We no longer use the 'B' word."

Progressive lenses. What a glorious description! It does not evoke visions of thick lenses in ghastly black frames. Progressive gives me the feel of growth, evolution, moving ahead, being a "with it" kind of woman. I have always wanted to be progressive. No longer was I intimidated or frightened. I had progressive lenses and I suddenly felt very youthful and cutting-edge.

I am a writer. I have the look. I have no disease of the eye. Life is good – I am progressive!

⌛⌛⌛⌛⌛⌛⌛

Regarding Forgetfulness . . .

Please allow me to ease your mind regarding a common misconception. Because of frantic lives, many of us – yes, even I – have difficulty remembering every appointment, meeting, event, phone call, or errand demanding our attention. Ours is a fast-paced life with a thirst for immediate satisfaction. We rely on microwaves, fax machines, overnight shipping, one-hour photo processing, and e-mail. Even with our timesaving gadgets, we are busier now than we have ever been.

With all these thoughts churning inside our minds, it is reasonable that we should occasionally suffer from what I have termed *Brain Overload*. There are persons, of course, not as enlightened as I who may confuse this classic condition with memory loss or forgetfulness, items generally attributed to the aging process.

Not so, dear friends! We are simply afflicted by the frantic pace of today's world and the countless demands placed upon us. The fact that *Brain Overload* occurs more often as we age is simply an unfortunate coincidence. As more demands are placed upon us, *Brain Overload* naturally occurs more often. This does not mean that we are becoming absentminded, scatterbrained or old. Nay! We are simply victims of society's rapid pace.

Are you experiencing *Brain Overload*? It is very likely that you have suffered one of its many forms. Train yourself to recognize the many varieties of *Brain Overload*. Education is power. Allow what you learn here to ease your mind as you gain more knowledge of this common ailment – the lamentable byproduct of a very busy life.

13

"Official To-Do List" Syndrome

Perhaps the most common strain of *Brain Overload*, addresses the unavoidable Official To-Do List.

Like everyone else, I have too much to do and too little time for doing it. Errands and ideas assail me from all directions and, to maintain my exceptional level of professionalism and competency, I faithfully record tasks on my Official To-Do List – a list that obviously eats fertilizer because it grows quicker than the weeds in my front yard.

This syndrome is further complicated because my encyclopedia-sized Official To-Do List is not always with me. So I am forever writing notes everywhere – on napkins, credit card receipts, church bulletins (let's not say anything to Dee Shelnutt, my minister, about notes on the church bulletin – I would rather him think I am jotting down profound thoughts derived from his sermon!), or any scrap of paper that happens to be in my presence. But, before I can transfer these vital notes to my Official To-Do List, I forget where I stuffed these scraps of paper containing information crucial to my life and career.

In fact, there have been times when I have even forgotten where I placed my Official To-Do List. And my Official Calendar! How pitiful that I cannot remember things without written reminders. How pitiful that I cannot even keep up with my written reminders.

Some would call my problem "forgetfulness" and blame it on my compilation of birthdays. Not so! This is merely "Official To-Do List" Syndrome, a dreaded strain of *Brain Overload.*

I admit that I did not require an Official To-Do List when I was younger, but I was not as busy then as now. Because of my role as a writer, speaker, singer, businesswoman, etc., I must remember deadlines, speaking engagements, phone numbers, story ideas, meetings, and so forth.

On occasion, I have even been known to schedule time for things as decadent as fun or rest.

No doubt, an Official To-Do List or calendar crammed with dates occupies your refrigerator door, desktop, organizer, or computer.

Rest easy, my friends. Your mind is still intact. Relax and recognize your problem for what it is – "Official To-Do List" Syndrome – a common strain of *Brain Overload.*

Be at peace. You are not alone.

"Why Did I Come In Here?" Syndrome

This strain of *Brain Overload* frightened me at first. Though I cannot recall when it began, I gradually realized that something strange was happening to me. I would walk into a room intending to locate or retrieve a certain item . . . a book, a shirt, or a glass of water. Upon reaching the room, though, I would stand in the doorway trying to remember my reason for entering the room.

"Why did I come in here?" I asked myself.

This is occurring with such frequency that I wonder whether I should carry my encyclopedia-sized Official To-Do List with me at all times. I could then write down my reason for entering a specific room, thus accomplishing the task at hand.

I had no intention of ever mentioning this condition until having dinner with a group of girlfriends one evening. Someone brought up the subject of aging and forgetfulness. This friend even mentioned that, from time to time, she would walk into a room for a specific reason and, upon arrival, forget why she even went into the room. Amazingly, almost everyone else in the group admitted to having the same problem. I did not feel compelled to share my own experience with "Why Did I Come In Here?" Syndrome. There was no reason. Just by talking together, we established that these happenings were quite common and nothing I could say would provide further enlightenment. I was simply happy to learn that others, none of whom were elderly, shared these episodes. This proves the premise that "Why Did I Come

15

In Here?" Syndrome is simply another annoying element of *Brain Overload.*

Are you having problems remembering why you enter a room? I believe I have sufficiently proven that aging is not the culprit.

Be at peace. You are not alone.

"Now What Is That Word?" Syndrome

A lesser-known breed of *Brain Overload* is one in which a certain word or phrase lingers in a back corner of your brain and will not come forward. No matter how hard you concentrate, this information refuses to travel to the part of your brain that desperately craves this certain word or phrase.

"Now What Is That Word?" Syndrome is especially frustrating for people like me who make a living by writing or speaking. The Syndrome attacks indiscriminately. At times I may be in my office, desperately seeking to meet a writing deadline. Though inconvenient and frustrating, at least I am in the privacy of my own workplace and can use a dictionary or thesaurus until the word gradually travels to the portion of my brain controlling my writing ability.

This problem is far worse when I am speaking before a large group of people. A word I desperately need may completely slip my mind. Hundreds of eyes stare at me while I have a communication, or lack-of-communication, meltdown. The stress of staring into a microphone only increases the brain's inability to supply the word I desperately seek.

I pray regularly that "Now What Is That Word?" Syndrome does not plague me often. In fact, I am willing to ceremonially burn incense before Webster's Dictionary and/or Roget's Thesaurus if this will increase my knowledge, wisdom, and vocabulary. The only thought that soothes my soul is recognizing that "Now What Is That Word" Syndrome is not age-related. It is merely due to the stress of meeting deadlines and speaking before large groups of people. Once again, *Brain Overload* has reared its ugly head.

I am comforted when I hear that other speakers and writers experience this same frustration. This reminds me that I am not developing a premature case of Alzheimer's or becoming just plain forgetful. This frustration afflicts everyone at some time or another.

Be at peace. You are not alone.

"Now What Is Your Name?" Syndrome

Same syndrome as above except that, instead of words, you cannot remember a name. This might be the name of a distant relative, a friend you haven't seen in years, or your spouse.

Be at peace. You are not alone.

"The Scavenger Hunt" Syndrome

On a typical day I make hundreds of trips throughout my home . . . back to front, east to west, patio to front porch, and every corner in between. This has nothing to do with cleaning, exercising, or even relishing my home. This daily tour of my home focuses on nothing in particular and everything in general.

Consider this. While working in my office I usually develop a hankering for an icy Caffeine Free Diet Coke around 10:00 a.m. Walking to the kitchen, I fill my glass and turn back to my office. Before leaving the kitchen I notice dirty dishes in the sink that need to be loaded into the dishwasher. Once I begin this chore I remember a glass in my bedroom that should be included with this load of dishes. I walk the length of my house to the bedroom and retrieve the glass, fully intent on placing it in the dishwasher right away. But, as I pick up the glass from the bedside table, I see the earrings I took off the night before – earrings that need to be placed inside my jewelry box.

My jewelry box is located atop my dresser and, as I place the earrings inside, I notice a bottle of hairspray on my dresser that actually belongs in the bathroom closet. As I walk through the bathroom with the hairspray, I notice my bathtub. It is definitely time to get rid of the ring around the tub but the cleaning supplies are under the kitchen sink at the opposite end of my house.

Forgetting the glass and the dishwasher, I walk to the kitchen where I see that the laundry door is ajar. There is laundry in the dryer that needs to be folded. Smelling the fresh, clean scent, I have a hankering to crawl between spotless sheets later that night. While I search the closet for bed linens to suit my mood, a pair of curtains falls from a top shelf. At last! I have been searching for these curtains for eons and want to put them in my living room – immediately. I iron the curtains then march into the living room where I notice a wobbly bracket over the left window. Now where is the screwdriver? I walk through the kitchen to the garage and locate a toolbox containing a variety of screwdrivers. Leaving the garage, I pass several boxes of books. Oh no! I forgot about a shipment of books going to a bookstore in Virginia. Because my books and shipping supplies are in the garage, I drop the screwdriver and begin counting books and packing them for shipping.

Of course, an invoice and shipping label must accompany the book order so I stroll back to my office where I prepare the paperwork at my computer. I begin to work but realize that I am really thirsty. Wow, an icy Caffeine Free Diet Coke would really hit the spot!

Putting the invoice on hold, I rush to the kitchen for something to quench the thirst I worked up while rushing from one end of my house to the other. On the way, I continually mutter to myself, "Do not look around – just go back to the office and get to work." As if wearing blinders, I actually return to my office and prepare the shipping label and invoice for the books going to Virginia.

By this time, it is almost noon and I feel tired and frustrated. How is it that it is practically lunchtime and all I have accomplished is preparing a box of books for shipping and drinking an icy Caffeine Free Diet Coke?

In frustration I sit at my desk and wonder why I cannot get more work done.

I find chores in every room. It is truly as though I am on a scavenger hunt – searching for ways to mark items off my Official To-Do List, tasks that await me in every corner of my house. This is *Brain Overload*, specifically the dreaded "Scavenger Hunt" strain.

Are you a victim?

Be at peace. You are not alone.

As you can see, *Brain Overload* has many forms. Surely you have been afflicted with at least one. Feeling absentminded? Forgetful? Scatterbrained? Is preoccupation with the many facets of your life causing you to feel a bit empty-headed?

The diagnosis is *Brain Overload*, my friends. You are a busy, popular person pulled in multiple directions.

Be at peace. You are not alone.

⌛⌛⌛⌛⌛⌛⌛

Regarding The Senior Citizen Discount . . .

So far, so good. To date no one has offered me a Senior Citizen Discount. At forty-six I am still a few years away from this perk. However, if one were offered, I would probably accept it just because of the insult it implies. Well . . . the insult plus the chance to save a few pennies.

The Senior Citizen Discount is usually available at restaurants, drug stores, grocery stores, etc., for those persons fortunate enough to have achieved ages upwards of fifty-five or more. These discounts add up and, if you are like me, you need all the financial assistance you can get.

Despite best intentions, there have been awkward times when Senior Citizen Discounts have been offered in error to those much younger than fifty-five or sixty. It will probably not surprise you to learn that men seem not to care. In fact, most take the discount and run. Likewise, it will probably not surprise you to learn that women react quite differently.

My research indicates three major reasons for the faux pas of offering a Senior Citizen Discount prematurely, perhaps while a person is still in his or her thirties or forties:

Reason #1. A bad day. Bad days occur for a wide variety of reasons. Your new car fails to start the day after you buy it. Your computer crashes just as you complete a 70-page document you forgot to back up. Your preschooler gets sick on the new suit you are wearing for a meeting with the company president. Your air conditioning dies on the hottest day of the year. You are late for a meeting at church and the gas gauge is on empty. Maybe your evil sister pays you a surprise visit while you have a ghastly case of bed head, are wearing no make-up, and cleaning a spot on the carpet where the dog had an accident. Oh, and it is past noon and you are still in your most hideous pair of pajamas.

Bad days cause clenched teeth, narrowed eyes, migraines, acid reflux or gastric disorders of an even more embarrassing nature. Your face contorts in frustration and, without realizing it, you really do look much older than you are.

It is important to realize that the cashier at the drugstore, grocery, or restaurant, does not know that the universe has conspired against you that day. The cashier is simply there to total your purchases and, if you look the part, to offer the Senior Citizen Discount. If the stress of the day has caused your skin to turn pasty, your brows to furrow, and your fine lines to look like canyons, you might actually look a tad older. At this point, watch out! The Senior Citizen Discount may accidentally be offered.

Reason #2. The person at the checkout counter is a prepubescent child who believes anyone past thirty is a Senior Citizen.

I once believed this myself so I really can't be too hard on the child working the register. He or she will be punished one day when they turn forty and realize how wrong they were. In due time they will have to face their own offers of Senior Citizen Discounts. We may not be around to see this but relax in the knowledge that, as sure as God made little green apples, all young smart alecks will receive their comeuppance.

Reason #3. You really do look old!

⏳⏳⏳⏳⏳⏳

Deborah Mason is a true sister to me, even though heredity did not make us so. She is one of my "family of choice," an exceptional friend who listens to my joys and frustrations. We gladly calm one another through whatever emotional meltdown we may be facing on a daily, weekly, or sometimes hourly basis. We talk so often, in fact, that I was quite surprised when several days passed before I learned about Deborah's first encounter with the dreaded Senior Citizen Discount.

I suppose it is quite traumatic when someone offers you a Senior Citizen Discount for the very first time – especially if you have not yet celebrated enough birthdays to quality for said discount. Although this has certainly not happened to me, I would probably take the discount and run, considering it proper payback for whatever youthful yahoo, heaven forbid, accused me of looking older than my actual years.

No so for Deborah.

She, to put it kindly and delicately, declined her discount.

Working for a large well-known company, Deborah has been caught up in a world hit hard by recent economic conditions. Her vocabulary has expanded to include terms such as "outsourcing" and "downsizing." Naturally, Deborah has been most concerned about falling victim to one of these terms, especially since she is a single mom with a growing son, Drew, whom we affectionately call "BP" – a loving yet descriptive abbreviation for "Bottomless Pit." Drew has the typical appetite of a growing young man so Deborah knows all shortcuts to the closest grocery store.

Deborah had a particularly trying day at work one Thursday a few years back. In addition to rushing to meet a looming deadline, wrestling with a new computer program, and attending two long and unproductive meetings, the uncertainty of the job situation weighed heavily on her mind. When 5:00 p.m. arrived, she rushed from the office, picked up Drew from his after-school program, and took one of those shortcuts to the nearest grocery store.

The strain of the day showed on her face as, dashing from aisle to aisle, she filled the shopping cart with food for that evening and the weekend. All the while she made a mental list of things that awaited her once she arrived home – preparing dinner, helping Drew with his homework, washing a few loads of laundry, and paying an ever-increasing stack of bills. These and other tasks had to be accomplished before she would fall into bed for a few hours of sleep before the alarm sounded at 5:45 a.m., signaling yet another day filled with its own challenges.

Filling her cart, Deborah rushed to the checkout counter. She did have a rather obvious case of clenched teeth and narrowed eyes. And, sure enough, the prepubescent child at the register thought her to be older than her forty-something years. With total innocence, he asked, "Ma'am, would you like your discount?"

Deborah shook her head in confusion. Discount? She wasn't aware of any discount available to her.

"What discount," she asked hurriedly.

22

"Well, ma'am, it's Thursday. You are entitled to a discount on Thursday," the cashier explained.

"What discount?"

"The Senior Citizen Discount, ma'am. Every Thursday Senior Citizens receive 10% off their purchase."

At this point, Drew added some new words to his vocabulary as Deborah declined the discount using rather colorful language. And I suppose it was the excitement of the moment or *Brain Overload* that caused Deborah to forget to relay this incident to me. Thank goodness for Drew who remembered all details of the story quite vividly. If not for him, I probably never would have known about Deborah's Senior Citizen Discount Incident.

Rumor has it that the prepubescent cashier left the grocery store that day and has never been heard from since.

As for Deborah, I've learned never to mention the "D" word to her again.

Regarding Gravity . . .

Sag. Bag. Drag. Gag!

Regarding Hormones . . .

Monsters! When these invisible demons take hold of your mind and body, you may feel an overwhelming need to dial 1-800-EXORCIST. Hormones are unpredictable, erratic, and evil little spirits that seem to enjoy causing everything from anxiety to zits. Hold on – it's gonna be a bumpy ride!

Puberty. The devil breaks loose and body parts develop, hair grows, voices change, and moods swing. You experience an overpowering assortment of thoughts and emotions. That guy that once made you sick suddenly grabs your attention. At times you feel like crying for absolutely no reason at all. With millions of other women, you utter those ghastly words: "You mean this is going to happen to me every 28 days?"

Your first crush ushers in a new way of life – dressing in clothes that attract the opposite sex, waiting on the telephone to ring, crying over rejection, feeling the elation of your first kiss.

You fall in love at sixteen and cannot understand why everyone says you are too young to be serious about one person. You love someone so much it hurts and you feel certain God intends for you to marry this perfect person as soon as you have your diploma in hand and march out of high school to the strains of "Pomp and Circumstance." You cry uncontrollably and believe life is over when your perfect romance, in due course, proves to be imperfect. Why does life have to hurt so badly?

Adulthood. The gynecologist. The mammogram. Weight loss. Weight gain.

"So, you think I have PMS? Why do you say that? Moody? I'm not moody, but I'll show you moody if you don't leave me alone. Just give me some chocolate and get out of my face."

A baby is on its way and the body develops a mind of its own. Morning sickness, swelling body parts, multiple bathroom trips, backaches, grumpiness, fluid retention, and puffy feet. You feel like crying for no reason at all.

Labor begins and a new life and new responsibilities enter your world. Epidurals. You should be happy but feel so sad. Postpartum depression? You wonder how long it will last and whether you will ever sleep again.

"Does my husband still find me desirable?"

"Will my wife ever leave the baby and pay attention to me again? Is romance over until the kids turn twenty-one?"

Men aren't supposed to cry. I thought only women had mood swings. Mid-life crisis. Gold chains. Convertibles. Receding hairlines. Rogaine. Suddenly someone hands you a brochure advertising The Hair Club for Men. What is all this fuss about the prostate?

"But doctor, I don't want to turn my head and cough. Wait! Is this really a prescription for Viagra?"

"Does anyone understand me?"

24

Aging. The hormones rage on. Night sweats, cramps, fatigue, thoughts of plastic surgery. You feel like crying for no reason at all.

"Is it just me or is it hot in here?"

You can't concentrate. Depression. Menopause. Hormone replacement therapy?

"This can't be happening to me – I'm still young!"

"Is it my imagination or does it look like I'm growing a beard?"

Regarding Facial Hair . . .

As mentioned before, I have at least part of this aging thing figured out. When it comes to hair, men do want it on their heads while women do not want it on their faces. Seems simple enough . . . but wait.

There is a time in a woman's life when certain hormonal changes take place. I am approaching this age and am exhibiting characteristics of something doctors call perimenopause, a stage where a woman's body is transitioning into actual menopause.

A rose by any other name . . .

By either name, it means your hormones are wacky and you are going to be wacky as well. Just like the real thing, perimenopause may include hot flashes, fatigue, irritability, and all the other nightmares often associated with this unique time of life. Because fatigue and irritability are typical symptoms, there are some who would believe I have been going through perimenopause all my life. A vicious lie! Thankfully, my hot flashes have been minimal. And I have had no more mood swings than usual – a frightening thought in itself. I can deal with these things. I have faced them before.

However, there is one characteristic of the perimenopause/menopause stage of life that, quite frankly, scares me to death. In fact, I have decided that I will simply have no part of it. Other women have encountered this phenomenon and have confronted it with grace and

25

dignity. But I shall not fall victim to this sure mark of growing older. In fact, these two little words have the power to render me speechless and send me into mourning for days . . . *FACIAL HAIR.*

The plain and simple truth is this – I did not come into this world with a beard and I will not leave this world with a beard.

As I mentioned, the fact that some women fall victim to the blight of facial hair does not bother me. On the contrary, I admire and respect them. Even some of my very best friends are struggling with this hormonal harassment.

Jennifer Huycke has been a special friend for many years. You may have read about her in my other books and articles. Our exploits are famous in these parts and we have shared many experiences in our lives. Thankfully, there is one matter I have not yet shared with Jennifer. Yea verily, Jennifer has been plagued with facial hair.

For the record, I have not.

And while we are best of friends, I do find some demented sense of pleasure in knowing that Jennifer must "face" this alone while I remain free from the stigma of facial hair. Of course, I would never, ever poke fun at my dear friend who carries several sets of tweezers in her purse. That would be unkind. Some scandalmonger even stated that Jennifer sleeps with a tweezers under her pillow. Who would participate in such nasty gossip? That would be heartless. And there is absolutely no truth to the rumor that I gave Jennifer a $50 gift certificate for waxing on her last birthday. That would be insensitive. Plus, it was only a $25 gift certificate.

But I will tell you a true story.

For years Jennifer and I have talked on a daily basis, sharing our closest dreams and secrets. Now that I am traveling quite often to various speaking engagements, I always call Jennifer when I am leaving town. I give her all pertinent information – the route I will travel, where I will stay, the location of the event. Of course, she has my cell phone number and can call at any time. She is my sister, in the best sense of the word, and I want someone in my family of friends to know where I will be.

I always end the conversation by saying, "Okay, if I get hit by a truck hauling hogs or fall off a mountain, you will know where to find the body. But, before you do anything else, go clean my house!"

She always promises to do this.

Recently, the Florida beaches were calling and Jennifer's family decided to answer. Packing for a family of four took several days for Jennifer and her husband, Dick. Their van was loaded with clothes, swimsuits, and toys for the children ranging from handheld computer games to floating rafts for the ocean. Oh, and a cooler the size of a small home was filled with snacks and drinks. As they were leaving early one Saturday morning, Jennifer realized one task remained on her Official To-Do List – Call Cathy.

My telephone rang early and Jennifer quickly began to babble.

"Do you have a pen and paper?" she asked.

"I'm ready," I responded.

Jennifer supplied me with pertinent information regarding their beach trip – the route, the hotel, and all appropriate details. She made sure I had all cell phone and beeper numbers.

I finally stopped her. "Don't worry – I have all the information."

"Well," she hesitated, "I do need to ask one last thing."

"Go ahead."

Jennifer spoke again, using words that sounded quite familiar to me.

"Now, if we get hit by a truck hauling hogs or fall off a mountain, I don't want you to worry about cleaning my house."

Well, that was a relief! I hardly have time to clean my own house. I thought the conversation had ended but Jennifer kept talking.

"There is something I want you to do that is more important than cleaning my house. Will you promise this as a solemn oath?"

Her words sounded rather ominous so I listened closely and could hardly believe what I heard.

"If we get hit by a truck hauling hogs or fall off a mountain (a mountain in Florida?), don't worry about my house," she repeated.

"You said that already."

"I know. Just listen and promise me you will take care of this very important matter."

As she began speaking, I could hardly maintain my self-control. In fact, I'm sure I was laughing hysterically before she ended her first sentence. Nevertheless, while Jennifer talked, I listened in amazement as I realized that, if my dear friend were to meet her end on a Florida roadway, she would not be concerned about family, friends, finances, and matters of the spirit. Nay! At the moment she crossed into the great beyond, Jennifer's thoughts would be on . . . *FACIAL HAIR!*

Should there be a tragic accident, I was asked to go immediately unto Florida and locate the bodies. Per Jennifer, I was to go to the funeral home and announce that I was the next of kin. Jennifer's final wishes included that I be swathed in black from head to toe. This color of mourning would indicate to all watching that I was deeply grieving for the loss of this beloved friend.

As Jennifer stated, "I want people to know I was popular."

"Okay," I agreed, "locate bodies and wrap myself in black. Should I practice weeping, wailing, and gnashing of teeth?"

I was kidding, but Jennifer liked the idea.

"Weeping, wailing and gnashing of teeth. That is perfect!" I could hear the smile in her voice.

I was instructed to grieve as never before. My cries should be heard as far away as New England and be so loud that the very foundations of the earth trembled. I was to carry an extra-large box of tissues, blow my nose regularly, and leave a trail of them throughout the funeral home. This is all in the name of popularity, of course.

Continuing her instructions, Jennifer asked that I continue my loud laments even as they wheeled the coffin into the viewing room. I was then to throw myself at the foot of the casket, crumpled, inconsolable, and prostrate with grief.

"Okay," I agreed, "A trail of tissues, loud laments, and I throw myself at the foot of the casket. I think I have it."

"Wait, I'm not finished," and she continued talking.

"Now this next part is perhaps the most important, so listen carefully."

"I'm listening," wondering what could possibly come next.

"After you have cried for 20 or so minutes at the foot of the casket, I want you to rise slowly and, without warning, fling – yes, fling yourself – into the very coffin."

Now Jennifer is my friend and these were her last wishes, but I did have my dignity to consider.

"Wait just a minute. I can claim the body, dress in black, weep loudly, and crumple to the floor in grief. But I simply cannot fling myself into the casket with you. People will get a very wrong impression of our friendship. That is asking a bit much, don't you think? Plus, do you know how short I am? I would have to get a running start in Canada in order to fling myself into your coffin."

"But you have to," Jennifer implored. "This is the most crucial part!"

"Why is this the most crucial part?"

"It is simple," she explained. "Once you leap over the edge of the coffin, I want you to locate a pair of tweezers you will have hidden in your black clothing. At that point, I want you to check me for chin hair!"

We laughed wildly.

But after that lengthy discourse, I simply could not let Jennifer have the last word. So I answered her.

"As your trusted friend, I will be glad to do that for you, Jennifer. Just let me know – which chin should I check!"

And so we are vain to the very end. But I do want to leave you with a calm mind. After sharing this story at a recent retreat, a woman approached me. Her husband worked in a funeral home and she simply wanted to inform me of one very important issue.

"Cathy, please tell Jennifer to be at peace tonight. Reputable funeral homes have a checklist of all items that must be addressed before a body is available for viewing. You will be relieved to know that FACIAL HAIR is on the checklist. Oh, and funeral home employees all have their own tweezers."

What an education I received that day. A checklist that includes facial hair. I did rest easier that night. Whenever the end comes, Jennifer will most certainly have her chin hair plucked. And I will no longer have to worry about flinging myself into her coffin.

Praise the Lord! I am at peace.

Regarding Weight...

I am swimming in a gene pool that includes short and fat. But I do not have a weight problem. No, sir! Weight jumps on me with no problem at all. In fact, this has been a lifelong dilemma and, no doubt, will continue for all the days I have left in this life. In addition to the genetic factor, I have had three knee operations and am limited in the exercise I can do. And I like cheesecake better than brussel sprouts. I don't know why. No one taught me to like the bad stuff better than the healthy stuff. It just came naturally.

When you are a child with a weight problem, you have to endure the insults and taunts of your peers. Some very unfortunate individuals even have to endure the insults and taunts of their own family. I find that extremely sad because I know people of all ages who are not accepted because of weight issues – good people who should not be judged solely on the basis of Barbie dolls and magazine covers.

I attended a class reunion several years ago and was surprised to find that a number of my aging classmates were facing their own battles of the bulge. Some of these very same classmates once teased and judged harshly when we were younger.

As mentioned, I am swimming in a gene pool that includes short and fat and, despite diets and exercise, I will fight a forever battle. So while I look very similar, many people my age look quite different from their high school and college days. They are just beginning to add the pounds and are in torment over past images that do not match what the mirror reflects.

Well, my mirror always reflected extra pounds. I wish things were different, predominantly because of health issues. But I am forty-six now and have far too much to do than pout about pounds.

I learned long ago that scales do not define who I am or measure my worth in God's eyes.

So I have dealt with the fat issues for many years, even as a child. I suppose that confirms my suspicion that I have always been ahead of my time!

Regarding Food...

In short, everything that tastes good is bad for you.

You can eat asparagus and cardboard. All other food raises your cholesterol, your triglycerides, hardens your arteries, causes cancer, hemorrhoids, and adds pounds.

So why are there Krispy Kreme Doughnut Stores that display the *"Hot Doughnuts Now"* sign? Why does Mick's Restaurant in Atlanta serve the best Oreo Cheesecake on the planet? And The Varsity the best onion rings? Why does Cracker Barrel offer fluffy biscuits with butter and jam?

I wish I knew the answer to these and many other baffling questions.

I only know that there had better be cheesecake in heaven because that is probably the next time I will get any.

Regarding sex . . .

Will someone please refresh my memory?

⧗⧗⧗⧗⧗⧗⧗

Life at any age is packed with many wonderful opportunities! Each stage brings its own celebrations and challenges. I believe the secret of it all is to keep faithful, keep loving, keep learning, and keep laughing.

Life is such a tremendous gift – every moment of it – yet I often pout when I should be celebrating. Where did I ever get the idea that life was fair and easy? I cannot answer that, but I have since learned that neither is true. Each day has its difficult and heartbreaking moments, but each one offers moments of wonder, too!

Help me recognize those moments, God, and to thank you for the gift of every moment, every day, every year, and every stage of my life. And when struggles seem overwhelming, dear Lord, remind me that dancing is acceptable at any age.

Party on!

Is not wisdom found among the aged?
Does not long life bring understanding?
To God belong wisdom and power;
Counsel and understanding are his.

-- Job 12:12-13

The Mind

The mind is its own place,
And in itself
Can make a heaven of Hell,
A hell of Heaven.

--John Milton
(1608-1674)
Paradise Lost

Cushioned toilet seats?
Give me an old hard porcelain seat.
I simply cannot get things
accomplished on a cushioned seat.
I feel as though I am about to
wet upon something that
ought not be wet upon.

And, if I occupy a seat so long
that cushioning
is required for comfort,
perhaps I am
just not ready to go!

Who? Me? Set In My Ways?

*N*ow that I am a world-famous (joke, get it?) writer/speaker/singer, I am often asked, "So, just what do you do all day?"

This question has become especially prominent since I took a step in faith and committed myself to this full-time ministry.

Some of my closest friends have no idea of what is involved in my work and cannot imagine how I spend my hours. And new acquaintances are completely baffled. Sometimes I am baffled myself because no two days are alike and each day usually holds enough work for several weeks. I am sure most people encounter this same frustration, whatever their job.

What I do each day is largely determined by whether I will be speaking, traveling, singing, writing, running errands, or attending meetings. Some days are filled with professional tasks such as answering e-mail, preparing programs, shipping books, organizing mounds of paperwork, and addressing countless items on my Official To-Do List. Other days are dedicated to personal jobs such as washing clothes, loading the dishwasher, pulling weeds from the front yard, or scrubbing the toilets.

And you thought being a writer was all glamour!

Glamorous or not, as soon as I complete one task, another awaits so I simply try to fill every hour. I recognize that mine is not the traditional 9:00 to 5:00 office job. I have held such jobs such in the past but, of course, I love the freedom and flexibility my current work allows.

Keeping in mind that no two days are alike, I will still try to answer the question at hand. Maybe, after reading this, my friends will have a better idea of how I spend my days and, as a result, will understand why I haven't answered their phone calls recently!

Cathy's "Typical" Day

❖ My typical day begins between 8:00 and 9:00 a.m. It is a well-documented fact that I am not a morning person. In fact, perky morning people (my friend, Janice, comes to mind) get on my very last nerve. Janice, for example, awakens with a song on her lips and happiness in her heart. She is more bearable once I smack her. I prefer to work late, usually until 1:00 or 2:00 a.m. I don't mind the late hours. Just let me sleep the next morning.

❖ Upon awaking, I make a mental list of the things I must accomplish that day. Then I seriously ponder how much longer I can stay in bed and still meet all my deadlines.

❖ Once I get out of bed, I go directly to the bathroom. (Yes, writers have to do that, too!).

❖ My second task is to turn on my main computer, log on to the Internet, and check for messages that may have dropped into my inbox while I slept. Though I go to bed late, there are still about fifteen messages awaiting me each morning. Far more arrive during the day. I read them and immediately answer those that are priorities. Good jokes are instantly forwarded to friends who share my demented sense of humor. Miscellaneous e-mails are put on hold until I complete my morning personal hygiene routine.

❖ The shower. I turn on the shower then brush my teeth while the hot water crawls all the way from the front of my house to the master bathroom. The timing is perfect because just as I rinse and spit, the shower is the correct temperature. I climb in and proceed with my customary routine – I wash my face. I wash my hair. I condition my hair. I wash the rest of me while the conditioner seeps into my hair follicles. I then rinse my hair. Stepping out of the shower, I cover my wet hair with a towel folded turban-style. I dry the rest of me with a second towel.

❖ Clothes are a must at this point, with my wardrobe based on my plans, my mood, and whether I have recently done the laundry. I put on fresh underwear (panties and a bra with a little pink rose on the front) just in case I should be in an accident.

❖ I towel-dry my hair and anoint it with mousse, gels, waxes, and spritz. I style it using a round brush with the dryer on the low setting. Because my hair is very fine and limp, I finish it off with a gallon of mega-spritz. The spritz gives me a fine case of what I have termed *helmet head* (very stiff hair), so that the style will hold until the cows come home!

❖ Make-up is applied. I sit before a lighted, magnifying mirror. This scares me more than you can imagine! I apply foundation, mascara (Lancôme waterproof), and other appropriate girly stuff. Mascara application is the most frustrating part of my morning routine. I have "eye-balds" and literally have to create eyelashes out of nothing! My make-up job takes much longer if I am going to speak and, hence, need to apply stage make-up.

❖ Once I am dressed with clean underwear and make-up, I might then run errands. But supposing this typical day includes working at home, this is when I turn off the TV or CD and park myself in front of my computer. I consult my Official To-Do List and address the things with stars beside them. There are always many stars. I answer e-mail, write letters, file for approximately 3.2 minutes before I want to scream because I hate filing. Once the screaming has subsided, I answer phone calls, pay bills, and try to organize the paperwork atop my desk. This takes approximately 2.2 minutes before I want to scream because I hate organizing paperwork. Once the screaming has again subsided, I check my calendar for upcoming retreats and/or speaking engagements and prepare for these events.

❖ At 11:00 a.m. I find work that will allow me to watch television for one hour. *The Practice* is in reruns on Channel 58 on my cable station and I allow myself a full sixty minutes to stare and drool over Dylan McDermott. Have you seen this guy? Hey, I'm human and a girl has gotta have something to brighten the day! By the way, anyone who locates and brings this man to my home will receive a free book and my eternal gratitude!

❖ Lunch is usually a grilled chicken Caesar salad (if I am good) or a cheeseburger (if I am bad). Note: It is a much easier to locate a cheeseburger than a grilled chicken Caesar salad.

❖ Afternoons are generally dedicated to writing. I have books and drawers filled with story ideas and I try to develop interesting stories for my books, columns, or web site. Writer's Block is a demon that usually seeks me out each afternoon, which I why I did not complete this book much earlier. But I write at least a page so that I can feel as though I have actually done something constructive to help keep a roof over my head.

❖ I normally break around 4:30 for an icy Caffeine Free Diet Coke.

❖ During my break I often do something really exciting like load the dishwasher or the washing machine. If I'm feeling especially frisky, I will scrub the shower or the bathtub.

❖ Returning to my desk, I tackle paperwork until approximately 7:30. By then I decide that I am hungry and wonder what to prepare for dinner. Prepare? I usually dismiss that idea and end up eating something that can be ordered at a take-out window. My domestic days are definitely behind me. Now I would rather work than cook.

❖ The evenings are dedicated to calling friends – Deborah, Mary, Lauren, Dee, Glenda, Jennifer, Jim, Gene, Mimi, or a variety of others. However, depending on the thickness of the pile, tackling more paperwork may be required. This is the time of day I would prefer to sit and enjoy a movie or read a book, but I feel guilty when I do that so I usually continue to work. Often I do meet friends for dinner. I have not yet met Dylan McDermott for dinner, but I do have my dreams.

❖ I continue working until 1:00 or 2:00 a.m. when I am definitely ready for bed.

❖ My nightly repertoire includes several steps as I prepare for a restful slumber. I remove all jewelry and locate a gown or pajamas to suit my mood. Sometimes I bathe in my big garden tub to ease the tension in my shoulders caused by facing a computer all day. I remove the three pounds of mascara on my eyelashes, wash my face with foam that promises to reduce fine lines, and then apply toner, moisturizer, and under-eye cream. I sprinkle myself with Johnson's Baby Powder because it smells good and makes me feel clean.

❖ Turning down the cover on my bed, I place my many pillows in a specific formation. I love being surrounded by pillows and burrowing beneath the covers. In fact, my late husband, Jerry, used to tell me: "Cathy, you don't sleep – you nest." I prepare the bed for my nightly nesting ritual. Two standard pillows are stacked on my right side. I then place a king-sized pillow lengthwise on top of the two standard pillows. Beneath my head is one standard pillow with another king-sized pillow resting atop it. One pillow goes under the cover for my feet because it just feels good. Two smaller pillows are spread about the bed for general snuggling purposes.

❖ The thermostat must be set to "frigidly cold." I sleep and nest much better when the temperature is cool.

❖ Because I will admit to being afraid of the dark, an array of nightlights fills my house. Each needs to be turned on. Ask my friends – if the lights go out, I immediately wake up. Yes, it is weird, but this is part of being me.

❖ Normally I sleep with the television turned on. It doesn't matter what is playing – I just have it on for the company. This habit began when my husband, Jerry, was in the hospital awaiting his heart transplant. I tried to sleep but could not because my mind would play the "what if" game. So I turned on the television and concentrated on whatever was playing instead of worrying about all the things that might happen to my husband. It helped me sleep and, over the years, became a habit. I usually set the station to NBC so that I can wake up with Katie and Matt.

❖ I drift off to a peaceful sleep with lights shining, the television playing, and the thermostat set to "Arctic Winter." I snuggle into the most comfortable bed on the planet and wake up between 8:00 and 9:00 a.m. the next day when the process begins again.

For those of you who have expressed an interest, I hope this brief outline provides insight into how I spend most of my days. I am just an average person with a non-traditional job. And, as mentioned, no two days are ever the same. I really enjoy the flexibility and variety.

Flexibility and variety! I am proud to say these are two positive character traits I possess. My goodness, you can easily see that from the schedule I just shared.

Yep, I am proud of the way I am handling this aging thing.

I might be growing older but, thank goodness, at least I am not set in my ways!

Whatever happens,
conduct yourselves in a manner
worthy of the gospel of Christ.

--*Philippians 1:27*

Direction Reflection

*N*aturally inquisitive, I have often wondered, "Just what do older people think about every day?"

From the start, let me state that I do not know the point at which one is considered "elderly." I would imagine it varies based on outlook and attitude.

However, most elderly folks I know are quite busy. Many hold part-time jobs or volunteer in various capacities. Though still busy, their frantic rush has slowed somewhat. No longer do they dash to a 12-hour a day job, prepare dinner each night for a growing family, or shuttle children from dance classes to soccer fields. For most, retirement means a slower pace and an opportunity to reflect on life's important issues.

So what occupies the mind of those who finally have the time to ponder the great questions of life? Are their thoughts mind-boggling or simply mundane? I mean, are elderly folks concerned that their clothes are chic or whether the car they drive will make them more popular than other elderly folks? Do they boast about their grandchildren or worry that certain clothes make them look fat? Do they consider the most recent BOTOX treatment or reflect upon matters of deep spiritual significance? Do they wonder about their various ailments and whether they will have time to do all the things they want to do in this life? Or do they simply question what to fix for dinner?

I ask these questions because of changes I have detected in my own way of thinking. At age five, my biggest concern was whether Santa would bring me a Thumbelina doll. By fourteen, I was deliberating how to tell a boy I liked him – hopefully without feeling the sharp sting of rejection. In college, I fretted over making an A in every class. Once I made the Dean's List, I thought I would surely die if I ever made a B again. After graduate school I fretted over where to work, where to live, and how to pay the bills. Then, of course, there were the gigantic matters of whether to marry, have children, and purchase a home.

I am still pondering life's great uncertainties and, being the inquisitive type, I always will. As I age, though, I am noticing a change in my priorities and, as a result, the questions I ask. Matters once vitally important – a Saturday night date, the model of my car, the accumulation of material things – hold little significance for me these days. As I grow older, I am grappling with topics of deeper importance, matters that leave my mind weary from intense contemplation.

Recently I have been wrestling with a subject that, to my knowledge, has never been definitively resolved, although it has been debated throughout the ages. In homes, businesses, hospitals, even churches, an answer has been sought for this pressing question. Opinions vary. But I do not want an opinion – I want an answer. Decisive. Uncompromising. Final.

My friends, I seek the ultimate answer to . . . *The Tissue Issue.*

Is toilet tissue directional?

What is the proper placement of toilet tissue on the bathroom cylinder? Over or under? Is there an authority on tissue etiquette that could, once and for all time, enlighten the public regarding proper Tissue Issue protocol. I believe I speak for a large majority when I state that we are weary of guesswork, conjecture, and the fear of being reported to the Tissue Police. Superior housekeepers everywhere demand a definitive answer.

Some may consider this a small matter, but I have an irrational fear that the Tissue Issue Police will raid my home, inspect each bathroom, and label me a disgraceful housekeeper. I would probably receive a Tissue Issue Citation and, before you know it, stand trial before a jury of Home Economics teachers who would pronounce me unworthy. Or perhaps, an army of photographers from *Home And Garden* magazine might, without warning, invade my home. Snapping pictures and taking notes, my domicile would become a feature article entitled, "Do You Want The Perfect Bathroom? Then Do Not Let This Happen To You!"

I want the proper bathroom. I do. I really do. So I must have an answer? Does the paper roll over or under?

Without benefit of an authoritative answer, I must rely solely on my own conviction. As you probably guessed, I indeed have an opinion regarding the Tissue Issue. So, for others struggling with proper bathroom etiquette, consider my thoughts.

In a word: OVER. The bathroom tissue should rotate above the top of the roll.

My opinion is unwavering. Why? Primarily, the tissue flows more smoothly as it traverses the summit of the spool. And it is far easier to locate the start of the roll when the paper rotates atop the cylinder. Otherwise, you will twist, bend, and contort in unnatural positions as you seek the elusive first sheet. Finally, I have actually done an unofficial survey and most of my friends and associates actually prefer their toilet tissue to advance from the top of the roll. Of course, this survey has not been certified by the Tissue Police, but I do believe the opinion of the majority should be binding until such time that a Tissue Authority provides additional facts.

The Tissue Issue has only recently begun to bother me. Quite frankly, I never considered the direction of toilet tissue when I was a child, a teen, or even a young adult. Please note that I do not know at what age one becomes a "young adult" or at what age one then moves into "middle adulthood." These are other matters that perplex me.

While I do not remember when I began to ponder the Tissue Issue, it has become quite significant to me in recent years. I observe the direction of toilet tissue when I visit schools, businesses, and even churches. The Tissue Issue inevitably arises when I visit with friends who are mature enough to handle a discussion of this magnitude. Bathrooms in their homes are impeccably clean and beautifully decorated. And, by far, the toilet tissue therein cascades over the top of the roll. Again, the majority has spoken so I respectfully conclude that Toilet Tissue is, indeed, directional – and the correct direction is OVER. Thus, it would seem that toilet tissue rotating UNDER the roll is an abomination and an affront to a civilized society.

As you can deduce, my Tissue Issue research has been thorough and painstaking. But in our world of uncertainty, there are questions that demand an answer. If I have helped educate a lost world, then the agony has been worth it all.

While I still do not know what occupies the minds of elderly folks, I am thankful only questions of great significance fill my mind. No doubt my questions will continue as I grow in years. After all, I am a deep thinker and would never waste my time on trivial notions!

With the Tissue Issue resolved, I must move forward. My next challenge? Shoes and socks. When dressing, should you completely outfit one foot with a sock and a shoe before moving to the second foot? Or should you place both socks on your feet, followed by both shoes? And do you start with your left foot or your right foot . . . .

Clearly, I want to make the world a better place and if I must struggle with life's uncertainties, I am ready. Lord, help me focus on the important things in life!

Therefore, holy brothers,
who share in the heavenly calling,
fix your thoughts on Jesus,
the apostle and high priest whom we confess.

--Hebrews 3:1

Road Kill Etiquette

No doubt about it – I am a country girl! I love the wide-open spaces, the fresh air, the green fields and dancing streams. Life in the country is also quite educational as you witness nature in action and the see the whole cycle of life in something as simple as an oak leaf.

However, life in the country can also raise fundamental questions.

It is obvious that my thinking is changing as I age because I never considered the subject of Road Kill Etiquette until a few years ago. Country lanes are forever littered with the remains of unfortunate critters that did not successfully cross the road. It is part of nature. But now that I am older and a responsible member of society, I am concerned with ecological and sanitation issues. Thus, it is time to ask the vital question: "What is proper Road Kill Etiquette?"

I seek truth, yet I do not know where to turn. Check the index of any book by Miss Manners. There is no mention of "road kill" or any subject remotely related to disposal of lifeless creatures on country roadways.

Lest you think I have gone completely mad, my concern with this subject began quite legitimately. While living in rural South Carolina several years ago, an unfortunate skunk met his demise at the end of my driveway. A hit-and-run driver took the life of a large skunk, and the ill-fated and odorous creature went belly-up on the highway at the end of my driveway – dead center of the road, sprawled across the yellow line.

47

Now, skunks were plentiful in those parts and, quite frankly, I was not sorry to see a dead one – unless, of course, the resting place of said skunk just happened to be the end of my driveway.

The skunk bothered me. Not just the odor, mind you, but the means of disposal. I am, after all, a curious type and my mind began to wander regarding the liability and disposal of said skunk.

Who was responsible? Was I?

I deliberated this matter for several days as the skunk grew, shall we say, increasingly ripe?

As stated, I was not the inconsiderate driver who bumped off said skunk. So why should I be responsible for the burial simply because the ill-fated and pungent creature rested at the end of my driveway? And how would I remove the animal without taking a bit of the skunk with me? I have heard horror stories about individuals having to bathe in tomato juice to rid themselves of long-lasting skunk perfume. I do not like tomato juice.

And how would I properly dispose of said skunk? Would I simply throw him into a ditch? Whose ditch? How far away should I move the hideous creature? Wherever I might take the animal, an overpowering odor would tell someone that a dead skunk was nearby. What is the proper distance for transporting a dead skunk? I could not imagine moving the skunk very far due to its potent aroma that made my eyes sting and my nose run. If proper etiquette required moving the skunk very far, that would involve placing it inside my car, which, I contend, would be a mistake of epic proportions. Once placed in my car, a reeking reminder of said skunk would no doubt remain with me for months, if not the entire life of my car.

I considered a dumpster. But, whose dumpster? It would not be very neighborly to drop such a unique gift into a dumpster belonging to a local business.

Or was the disposal of said skunk the responsibility of David Gibson who lived across the road from me. The skunk was, after all, in the middle of the highway, extending equally across the yellow centerline. The skunk, therefore, could just as easily have belonged to David as to me. While said skunk was positioned at the entrance of my driveway, he also lay directly in front of David's house. Did the location of the skunk confer disposal rights to David or to me? I fretted these details carefully yet found no easy answer.

David Gibson is one of the finest men I have ever met and while I did not wish to stick him with a foul and putrid chore, David is, after all, a man. And though I have strong convictions regarding the equality of women, I am old-fashioned enough to believe that skunk disposal should be the responsibility of the male of the species. I will gladly wash an extra load of laundry and cook a nice meal just to keep myself from having to dispose of an ugly, smelly skunk. Should my opinion reverse the Women's Movement by fifty or so years, so be it. I am talking about a skunk, okay?

Though David and I were the ones most inconvenienced by said skunk, I firmly felt that disposal should, without question, have been the responsibility of "the hitter." Shouldn't the driver of the vehicle that murdered the animal be responsible for its proper burial? This seemed quite fair to me, unless, of course, I were to hit a skunk. Unfortunately, "the hitter" had long fled and obviously had no intention of returning to the "scent" of the crime.

I thought about the DOT or Highway Department. Was there a Road Kill Crew specifically designated to rid our highways and byways of nuisances such as this? As a side bar, who might comprise the Road Kill Crew? Would one be elected to this position or possibly assigned to it as some form of extreme punishment? Furthermore, who would serve as President of the Road Kill Crew and would this be viewed as an honor or badge of shame?

Ultimately I concluded that we should simply leave the dead skunk in the middle of the road and let nature take its proper course. After all, God created buzzards and other scavengers who need to eat something. Would I be disturbing the natural food chain if I interfered and moved the skunk to an undisclosed location – although, based on the smell of it, the location would not remain undisclosed for very long!

I was perplexed and in distress over the dead skunk at the end of my driveway. I went to college! I made good grades! Yet I could not resolve the problem of skunk removal on a country road. What good was my education?

After developing an ulcer and suffering several sleepless nights, I finally followed the path of least resistance and let the skunk rest in peace right on the yellow line of the highway. If anyone asked, I decided I would stick with the "I'm not disturbing nature" story. Even though the decision was made, I still could not rid myself of the awful feeling that my neighbors were talking about me and looked upon me with contempt because I lacked knowledge of proper Road Kill Etiquette.

Oh, the struggle. Oh, the heartache. Oh, the joy I felt as on the fourth day following the tragedy, I watched dear David load the smoldering skunk remains into an old sack, place them on the back of his truck, and drive them deep into the woods. To this day, he remains my hero!

Even though the skunk situation was finally resolved, questions still haunt me – no, not questions regarding Road Kill Etiquette. That has passed. The question that concerns me now is, "Why did I spend so much time worrying about a dead skunk in the middle of a country road?"

Is this the sort of thing that preoccupies an aging mind? Perhaps I am getting old.

Or perhaps I am just disturbed.

> *The Lord knows the thoughts of man;*
> *He knows that they are futile.*
>
> *-- Psalm 94:11*

To Reflect the Heavens

*T*he sea is calm tonight – a striking image, completely calm with barely a ripple on its glossy surface. A few modest waves sashay toward the beach and greet the white sand with a soft, tender kiss. The water resembles polished glass or smooth, silky ice awaiting a skater who will slide, glide, leap, and carve delicate designs into its awaiting surface.

Though I have seen the ocean countless times, I never cease to be astonished by its unrivaled beauty and majesty. Like me, the ocean displays an array of personalities. At times the water rises and falls rhythmically and practically dances toward the shoreline. The brilliant aqua blue rolls onto the sand and leaves behind gifts of colorful shells and dark driftwood. There are other days, though, when waves reel and spin as the murky, agitated water leaps onto the beach, pushed by the ferocity of angry winds and a coming storm. Though the sea has many qualities, tonight it is wonderfully peaceful and quietly beautiful.

The sky above is just as glorious. Its gray blue canvas is decorated with colorful hues. A deep fuchsia just above the horizon highlights the spot where the sun is setting. The remainder of the buttermilk sky is filled with cotton-candy tufts of pinks and purples mixed with a million blue highlights. In the twilight of the day, the winter sky changes with each passing second, but each view has a magnificence all its own.

Standing next to the water, I feel the cool dampness on my face. A chill fills the winter air and I pull my sweater closer to me. Still, I am reluctant to leave this place that so obviously demonstrates God's reality and handiwork. There is a sense of peace here that I have not felt in such a long time. I want that peace to journey with me but I know that frustrations, deadlines, worries, and questions await me when I leave. Yet night is coming . . .

I take one last lingering look and can no longer perceive the distant rim of the ocean. Motionless, the water perfectly reflects the dazzling sunset and buttermilk sky suspended above. Though disconnected, the two appear united and I can no longer distinguish the ocean from the heavens. This great expanse surrounds me, a boundless jumble of blues, pinks, and purples reaching far to the horizon. The world seems endless. I feel disoriented because the sights above me are a mirror image of the sights before me.

And I feel like a tiny speck of insignificance amid the enormity of God's creation.

Yet I am anything but insignificant. I am part of creation and part of this glorious moment. Just as the quiet sea reflects the sky, I am to reflect the holiness and mighty power of God. Created in his very image, I am to show his love to others through my words as well as my life. Even my many flaws and imperfections may be used to show God to others

Despite these flaws and imperfections, I may be the only face of God some people see. What an awesome responsibility – not simply to reflect God but also to give witness to the way the world was meant to be . . . on earth as it is in heaven.

The enormity of the moment is life-changing! While witnessing the splendor of creation, I hear the very voice of God in the wonder of it all.

"Look closely," God softly speaks. "Look closely and be like the ocean. Whether the days are peaceful or filled with stormy anxiety, you are to be calm and at peace. And like the mighty ocean – whether tempestuous or quietly serene – you are to reflect the heavens in the things you say or do."

St. Francis of Assisi penned some of my favorite words, simple in speech but profound in meaning:

"Always be a witness for Christ;
If necessary, use words."

Be still. Be silent. Listen for God's whisper amid the storms and the gentle calm days of your life. He speaks to you as he speaks to me.

Whatever your age . . . whatever your circumstance . . . whatever your flaws or imperfections, seek to find God in the beauty of creation. Worship him in that moment. Then with confidence and the peace only God can provide, go forth to reflect the heavens.

But just as he who called you
is holy,
so be holy in all you do;
For it is written:
"Be holy, because I am holy."

--1 Peter 1:15

The Body

As we grow old,
the beauty
seals inward.

--Bronson Alcott
(1799-1888)

Wow!

*I never expected
my chest
and
my belly button
to
occupy the same space.*

Just Call Me "Two-Faced"

My face melted on a Saturday. Well, not my entire face – just the right side.

For weeks the paperwork on my desk had grown faster than kudzu on a quiet country road. It demanded my attention and I assumed the calm of a Saturday morning would provide time to obliterate the wicked stuff. After working feverishly for two hours, I felt a strange tingling below my right bottom lip. The feeling gradually intensified. Suddenly I had an odd sensation – almost as if the skin on the right side of my face was melting – dropping helplessly into the shirt I was wearing.

Scared? You bet I was. My right eye would not blink correctly and my lips contorted strangely when I tried to rub them together. My mind raced. Was I having a stroke? Had I suddenly developed some abnormal disease? Was I having an allergic reaction to something? Were these colossal piles of paperwork emitting "face melting" fumes? What was happening to me?

Whatever it was, I decided to leave the office. There were others in the building, but I managed to leave through a side door without seeing anyone.

"If I am having a stroke," I strangely reasoned, "I am going to do it in the privacy of my own home."

Yes, I can be quite stubborn!

I am thrilled to report that I did not have a stroke that Saturday morning. The diagnosis was Bell's Palsy. Often caused by trauma or inflammation, Bell's Palsy affects a nerve at the base of the brain, causing weakness or paralysis of facial muscles. A virus may also cause the cursed condition. In cases such as mine, the body may carry a virus that remains dormant until triggered by stress or fatigue.

Bell's Palsy strikes approximately 40,000 individuals each year. It is not uncommon and I know others who have experienced the frustration and anxiety of Bell's Palsy. Having some knowledge of this infirmity helped me realize that I probably was not experiencing a stroke. Nevertheless, the event was still very frightening as the symptoms worsened during the early hours of onset.

My doctor calmed me as he explained that my irritating problems were indeed related to a cranial nerve that simply fizzled – just like a wire shorting out. This same nerve controlled the muscles on the right side of my face. Thus, I would not regain control over these muscles until the nerve began to heal itself.

"How long will this last, doc?" I asked impatiently. "I would like to be healed by morning. If you will just give me a pill, I will be on my way."

No such luck! Unfortunately, my doctor spoke words that I simply did not want to hear. There was no quick fix. While the vast majority of sufferers ultimately experience a complete recovery, it is not immediate. Healing takes time. Depending on the person and the circumstances, a complete recovery can take from one to six months.

"Cathy," he said softly, "this is going to teach you patience."

"But I don't want to be patient," I whined. "Make it go away now!"

What I wanted, though, made no difference at all. The fact was that I had Bell's Palsy and there was no pill or immediate cure. I could not wish it away or speed up the healing process by being impatient or angry. I had no choice but to wait until the nerve healed and would, once again, have the ability to control my facial muscles.

Though my symptoms worsened that first day, by the following day they stabilized. All I could do was wait . . . and to learn to live with only half my face in proper working order.

My right eye would not blink. And it would not remain closed at night. I purchased first aid supplies to tape my eye shut each night before going to bed. Without this safeguard, my eye would remain open while I slept and all sorts of lint and allergens would hop right in and cause infection. I certainly did not need an infection so I opted to go to bed each night looking somewhat like Long John Silver. All I needed was a parrot on my shoulder to complete the ensemble.

The right side of my mouth drooped, creating a lopsided smile and an array of interesting problems. Routine dental hygiene became comical. Brushing my teeth was not so bad, but rinsing was quite a challenge. On that first night – and for the next eight weeks or so – water shot out of the right corner of my mouth when I swished and rinsed. My mouth simply would not close properly and a geyser-like stream of water blasted through my lips. I felt like Old Faithful. (Of course, there have been many times in my life when my mouth failed to close properly, but that material is for another book.)

My crooked mouth also presented a dilemma when I tried to eat or drink. I could only chew properly on my left side, so those teeth did double duty. I quickly realized I needed a straw for drinking purposes. Without one, liquid dribbled down my chin and neck, then entered the shirt where my face was hiding. Rushing to Wal-Mart, I bought a pack of bright neon straws and learned to drink by placing a straw in the left corner of my mouth while holding the right side of my mouth closed with my hand. Needless to say, I stayed close to home during these moments lest people wonder whether I should be institutionalized.

Talking on the phone was a nightmare and, at that time, I answered all calls at my office. Speaking with a melted face is no easy task. It was difficult enough to converse with customers face to face. However, customers who called our office must have thought I had developed a sudden fondness for the bottle –

and I don't mean the Coke bottle! I slurred and stammered as I answered the phone and greeted clients. The harder I tried, the more jumbled my speech became. Some words sounded fine if I spoke slowly. Most, however, were completely unintelligible. My frustration grew daily as I stumbled over the simplest of terms. Phrases I had used all my life had become enormous challenges that caused me to cry in aggravation.

As my words faltered one day, I realized in horror that I sounded akin to Charlie Brown's faceless and enigmatic schoolteacher. Remember her? She only knew one word – *Wah.* This mysterious educator only spoke in shades of *Wah.*

"Wah, wah, wah, wah, wah," she uttered as she asked Charlie Brown a question.

Though Charlie Brown responded with actual words, his teacher never veered from her one-word discourse.

"Wah, wah, wah, wah."

I once thought she was funny.

As the Bell's Palsy continued, I no longer saw the humor in the situation. I never wanted to be Charlie Brown's one-word teacher. In fact, I developed a personal disdain for this woman who, no doubt, suffered from a permanent case of Bell's Palsy.

Whether in an act of mercy or an effort to save the business, my co-workers began answering the phone for me.

Regardless of their kindness, my patience was waning. I was tired of looking like Long John Silver, spewing water like Old Faithful, and sounding like a one-word cartoon character.

My saving grace was a vast circle of friends who were tolerant and supportive, even though I was a tad testy. In fact, several of them mentioned something that surprised me. Even though I was frustrated, angry and irritated, those negative emotions did not register on my face. The lack of muscle control, oddly enough, prevented the right side of my face from frowning, wrinkling and showing signs of anxiety. Gone were furrowed brows, squinting eyes, and pursed lips. Nervous creases disappeared from my forehead, eyes, and jaws. According to some, the right side of my face looked five years younger than the left side.

Oh, the irony! Though I had prayed for wrinkles and creases to magically disappear, this irritating illness was most certainly not the cure I had in mind! Nevertheless, I tried to concentrate on the blessing of looking five years younger – at least on my right side.

Gradually, though, the healing began. I no longer had to tape my eye closed at night. Water did not spew like Old Faithful when I rinsed and swished. I even began to regain control over my words and my drooping mouth. I sounded less like the Charlie Brown "Wah Wah Queen" and more like myself. But, just as the doctor predicted, the healing took about three to four months.

My doctor also warned me of a possible complication of Bell's Palsy – synkinesis. This is a fancy word for problems that may arise as a patient recovers. As the nerve heals, some of the internal wiring may become crossed. Think of a thick cable that is comprised of many different small wires. If the cable is broken, there is no guarantee that each tiny wire will reattach to its proper partner. In other words, as the nerve regenerates, certain nerve fibers may reconnect to the wrong muscle. Some tiny fibers may break and never bond to the proper muscle part again. Thus, though the brain sends a command to a certain area of the face, the corresponding action may occur elsewhere.

I did experience synkinesis during my recovery and can truthfully say that some of my wires are crossed! For example, my right eye sometimes will not open as widely as my left eye. And if I rub my lips together, my right eye winks. Hey, it has gotten me a date or two! The doctor tells me that I now have a built in "Stress and Fatigue Detector." If I work too hard or become too anxious, the right side of my face will begin to feel weak and is a signal for me to slow down and get some rest. If these are the only idiosyncrasies I experience from my unfortunate face-melting episode, then I am quite thankful.

When this weakness arises, I easily recall the frustration of living with Bell's Palsy. So many things I took for granted were incredibly difficult at that time. Simple one-syllable words

61

became overwhelming obstacles. Basic speech required tremendous effort due to a tiny damaged nerve and the resulting loss of muscle control. My brain and sagging mouth were not collaborating and speaking even the simplest word was not worth the effort.

We all face times when words fail us. And Bell's Palsy cannot be blamed when our hearts and mouths do not collaborate and words that heal and restore remain unspoken. How uncomfortable it is to say, "I'm sorry." How agonizing to utter, "Forgive me." How painful to admit, "I made a mistake." And how frightening it can be to whisper, "I love you." Yet these three small syllables have the power to transform our lives and our world.

We are silenced by pride, fear, unfaithfulness and an unwillingness to utter words of love and forgiveness. So relationships falter and die. Husbands and wives divorce. Families disintegrate. Children carry grudges. Friendships fade. Countries go to war. Churches suffer and split.

And still, words of love and healing remain unspoken.

How easy it would be to blame these troubles on a frazzled nerve and crooked mouth. That would mean harsh words were beyond our control. But we hold the ultimate responsibility for the words we speak. And we are not alone. For centuries individuals have struggled with speaking kind words. Even the Gospels address this timeless battle: "Whoever would love life and see good days must keep his tongue from evil and his lips from deceitful speech" (I Peter 3:10).

Except for my complications from synkinesis, the Bell's Palsy incident is behind me. Just as my doctor predicted, my face "de-melted" after several months. There is no tape over my eye, the bathroom remains dry when I brush and rinse, and I can drink without use of a plastic neon straw.

Healing a broken relationship may take much longer. Some may never be healed at all unless we allow our hearts and mouths to collaborate and speak words that, though small, have the power to changes lives:

I'm sorry.
Forgive me.
I made a mistake.

I love you.

Dear God, you know that I cannot do this alone. Please help me speak your words – words that are often hard to say because my mouth and heart seem to be going in different directions. Take hold of my crooked mouth, Dear Lord, straighten my heart and help me to say only the words you would have me to say.

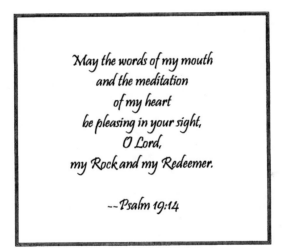

*May the words of my mouth
and the meditation
of my heart
be pleasing in your sight,
O Lord,
my Rock and my Redeemer.*

--Psalm 19:14

When given the opportunity,
never, ever
under any circumstance,
should you
pass up a chance
to go to
the
bathroom.

The Language of Aging

*J*ane Lathem is one of my favorite people. I love her because she is fun to be with. We can talk about anything – topics that have us crying one minute and laughing uncontrollably the next. Jane has a deep abiding faith and a strong sense of humor. She needs both. She is a minister's wife.

Her husband, Dr. Warren Lathem, is also one of my favorite people. He is one of the finest pastors I know, dedicated to his work yet smart enough to know not to take some things too seriously. Like Jane, Warren has a deep abiding faith and a strong sense of humor. He needs both because, well, he is married to Jane!

I have known Jane and Warren for many years now and we have cried and celebrated together during a heap of good and bad times. They are terrific friends – the sort I could call at 2:00 in the morning if I needed a comforting word. A friendship such as this is one of the treasures of aging.

With all her gifts and abilities, I especially cherish Jane for other reasons dear to my heart – she likes to talk and she likes to eat! Just like me! To enjoy both, Jane and I usually go to lunch together every few weeks. The place doesn't really matter because the menu always offers something delicious. What matters most is the friendship, the sharing, the laughter, the support . . . and that Jane is older than I.

(Will our friendship survive this story? Stay tuned!)

On a recent outing, I picked up Jane at her house. As soon as she entered my car, the conversation began. You see, Jane and I have one other thing in common – knee surgery. I have had three operations, but Jane had the most recent one. During her recovery, Warren presented her with a beautifully-colored cane. It was imported from some distant land and was the envy of anyone who ever had knee surgery in these parts. The wood was a dark tone adorned with striking designs in purple and green. For a while, it was Jane and the cane. They were always together.

However, on this particular day Jane walked to the car minus the infamous cane. I was impressed and happy for her, but I wondered about the cane.

"I'm flying solo today," she bravely explained.

I remembered my own knee surgeries and the aggravation of crutches and canes. I remembered the feeling of freedom that came when I finally walked unassisted. Those were red-letter days.

"I'm so proud of you!" I gushed. "We should celebrate. Let's eat!"

We shared our common knee experiences as we rode to the restaurant. The conversation included topics such as arthroscopy, ligaments, tendons, arthritis, and cortisone shots. Before we realized what was happening we had moved beyond the knee and were discussing wide-ranging aches and pains. We spoke of muscle relaxers, heating pads, ointments, balms and old country remedies. The conversation snowballed. We were out of control. Words such as cholesterol, triglycerides, blood pressure (both systolic and diastolic) and fluid retention decorated our dialogue. Suddenly, we began the hard stuff – hot flashes, night sweats, cramps, menopause, THE CHANGE!

At almost the very same moment, we looked at each other and screamed.

"Holy Methuselah, Batman, we are talking like old people!" I wailed.

Jane and I were only minutes away from our destination before we realized we had talked during the entire trip about our various ailments, twinges and spasms. We were becoming what we pledged never to become – old people with ailments! Even worse, we were becoming old people who actually enjoyed talking about our ailments. What had happened to us?

Suddenly we were afraid. Very afraid. We quickly changed the subject to something more constructive.

"So, got any good gossip?" I asked.

⧗⧗⧗⧗⧗⧗⧗

There does seem to be an exclusive language that comes with aging. One day you are talking about a first date or a new car then, BANG, the conversation suddenly switches to backaches and rheumatism. At the risk of sounding like an old person who does enjoy discussing my ailments, it is very important to stay up to date with the language of aging.

Why? Consider this.

I once knew a woman who worked in the office of a kidney specialist in the Atlanta area. This doctor was so popular it was almost impossible to secure an appointment with him. Most of his patients were referrals from other doctors who did not specialize in disorders of the kidney. Due to this doctor's distinguished reputation, his patients came from all areas of the southeastern United States.

One unforgettable patient was an older man from rural Alabama. This gentleman, let's call him Mr. Thompson, was highly respected in his hometown and an usher and deacon at the First Baptist Church. A farmer all his life, this fine man was very skilled in growing cotton, milking cows, and driving his John Deere tractor. Mr. Thompson developed a very serious kidney ailment and his local Alabama doctor referred him to this Atlanta specialist. With his wife and daughter, Mr. Thompson drove to the biggest city in the south, famous for its tall buildings and spaghetti-like system of roadways.

What a change from the rural area where he lived all his life. Though very self-assured in his hometown, Mr. Thompson was understandably intimidated by the fast pace, the traffic, and the size of the city. He was also intimidated by the maze of offices, parking decks, labs, medical equipment, and the large number of people dressed in white coats and scrubs near the doctor's office. It is understandable that he was quite jittery by the time he found the correct building, parked his car, and located the doctor's office.

What a relief to finally be in the proper location. He relaxed a bit and felt that the worst was behind him.

No such luck!

Enter Nurse Bertha Stoner.

Dressed in a crisp white uniform that matched the hair she pulled back into a tight bun, this no-nonsense woman seemed part grizzly bear and part army sergeant. Her voice had the bark of a Rottweiler and it was obvious that Nurse Bertha Stoner probably failed her class in "Compassionate Bedside Manner 101."

With clipboard in hand, Nurse Stoner advised Mr. Thompson that she needed to obtain his medical history. With an air of superiority, she spewed forth deeply intimate inquiries in rapid-fire succession. Though Mr. Thompson was fraught with embarrassment, Nurse Bertha Stoner proceeded with cold efficiency. If he paused to consider an answer, Nurse Bertha Stoner reminded him, "Sir, I have other patients waiting. You do realize you are not the only one who needs to see the doctor today."

This country gentleman wanted nothing more than to return home, slip into his well-worn overalls and forget he had ever met this demon of a woman. Nevertheless, he prevailed and answered all questions as correctly and quickly as possible.

As the interview ended, Nurse Bertha Stoner announced that she had just one final question. Mr. Thompson began to breathe easily just as Nurse Bertha Stoner suddenly threw him a curve ball.

"Mr. Thompson, have you had a BM today?"

A BM?

Mr. Thompson was dumbfounded. This gracious man and distinguished usher and deacon did not know how to answer this bizarre question. What was a BM? And had he actually had one? He had never heard such a term in his almost 70 years. He was dazed and unable to answer the question.

Her impatience showing, Nurse Bertha Stoner asked the question again in a louder voice. "Sir, this is a simple question. Have you experienced a BM at any time today?"

He glanced toward his loving wife, praying that she understood the question. Mrs. Thompson shrugged and looked as confused as her husband.

Meanwhile, Nurse Bertha Stoner impatiently tapped her clipboard with an ink pen.

"Mr. Thompson, would you please answer the question. It is very simple. Have you had a BM today?"

Still confused, Mr. Thompson summoned all the courage he possessed, looked straight into the face of Nurse Bertha Stoner and responded to the best of his ability.

"No, ma'am," he stammered. "I do not believe I have had a BM today. But I did have an RC at lunch."

Nurse Bertha Stoner, clipboard and all, turned on the heel of her white shoe and stormed out of the office without a word. Mr. Thompson glanced at his wife, assuming that he had answered the BM question correctly. He had no idea that Nurse Bertha Stoner was incensed at what she believed to be impudence and a complete lack of respect for her position.

I never met Mr. Thompson but I love that man! He was simply out of his comfort zone. Though a very smart man, he did not know the definition of a BM. No doubt, Nurse Bertha Stoner would be equally lost if asked to sow a field of cotton or climb aboard a tall John Deere tractor.

Can you see now the importance of remaining up to date regarding the vocabulary of aging?

You should be aware of the language your health care professionals are speaking. When your health is at stake there is no room for error.

I have never met Mr. Thompson but I love him! Any man that can maintain his dignity while removing Nurse Bertha Stoner from a room is a hero in my book.

You are a jewel, Mr. Thompson. Have an RC and put it on my tab!

> *The quiet words of the wise*
> *are more to be heeded*
> *than the shouts of a ruler of fools.*
>
> *--Ecclesiastes 9:17*

Upper Arm Emancipation!

*A*fter years of self-imposed bondage in long sleeves, short sleeves, and quarter-length sleeves, my upper arms were suddenly and unceremoniously emancipated in June 2002. Why? The thermometer read 107 degrees!

Thousands of women share my upper arm predicament. Age, weight, and gravity unite to wreak havoc with this body region. Though I cannot recall the specific time or day, long ago I said good-by to sleeveless dresses, cool summer blouses, and bright tank tops. There was good reason. My upper arms developed a personality all their own.

One of the most treasured members of my family is Katie Johnson, currently a student at Clemson University. (Go, Tigers!) She is learning Sign Language for her degree in Special Education To The Profoundly Handicapped. I admire Katie for many reasons, including her compassion, her courage, and the course of study she has chosen. I admire the way she uses her hands in beautiful rhythmic motion to speak and communicate. I spend a great deal of time with the Johnson family – Mary, Phil, Kaden, plus Katie's boyfriend and my buddy, Joey. During our times together, Katie has taught me a few simple words in sign language. It is fascinating and I want to learn more.

But I certainly never expected my upper arms to speak sign language – and with virtually no training at all.

Nevertheless, every time I lifted my arms to make a gesture, write on a blackboard, or even hug a small child, my

71

arms began to talk. With a wiggle, a flop, or a jello-like shake, my arms were in business for themselves. I could not control their erratic movement. Even more frightening, I had no idea of what they were saying! Were they giving a "come hither" message to a lecherous old geezer on the street? Were they instructing one of my dearest friends to go straight to the devil? Even worse, what if, by some stroke of fortune, I finally met Dylan McDermott and my arms told him, "Be gone, ugly man – you are not wanted here!"

Thus, the bondage began. I imprisoned my upper arms beneath an infinite collection of styles and fabrics. The arms were banished. No longer would they live unfettered and free. No longer would they enjoy cool summer breezes or bask in the warmth of sunlight. The risk was too great. The possibilities for unintentional insults were endless! Plus, I was completely embarrassed by the wobble and wiggle of skin that I could no longer control. So my upper arms turned lily white, never again to see the light of day. They became depressed inside their top-security prison of fabric. Their self-esteem suffered. My only consolation was knowing that I did not face Upper Arm Bondage alone. Thousands of women around the world suffered with me.

But this changed on that noteworthy day in June 2002.

You see, I am member of the United Methodist Church. These Methodists meet every summer for Annual Conference to conduct the business of the church and appoint ministers to serve the many congregations in our North Georgia Conference. I look forward to seeing friends from various churches each year, but I never look forward to the hot summer temperatures. To make matters even worse, Annual Conference 2002, was held in Augusta, Georgia (a seriously hot city) during June (a seriously hot month). Along with everyone else, I was boiling. And I grew even warmer when I noticed the 107-degree temperature reading on the outside thermometer. The air conditioning within the Civic Center was working frantically to cool the throng of sweaty, uncomfortable Methodists. But even an air conditioning unit the size of a small country can only fight so hard when the outside thermometer registers 107 degrees. The large crowd only added to the rising temperature inside the Civic Center.

To make matters worse, this was the first day of Annual Conference when everyone dons their best suits, complete with jackets fitting snugly over long-sleeved shirts or blouses. Seated at a display table near the main door, I cringed each time the door was opened, allowing precious bits of cool air to escape. Sweat droplets trickled down my back. I was one seriously sizzling Methodist!

"If these temperatures are a preview of hell, I am going to really start behaving myself," I advised Mimi, my cohort who accompanied me on this promotional trip.

Obviously, the immediate issue at hand was to cool myself. I prayed that a freak summer snowstorm would befall Augusta in spite of the purgatorial heat. Somehow I doubted my plea would be granted, so I considered a drastic measure.

My attire that day was an ankle-length tank-top dress covered by a navy blue jacket. The sole purpose for the jacket was to conceal my temperamental upper arms – the same upper arms that had not seen the light of day in decades. Did these body parts still speak their unique sign language? I did not know because they had been imprisoned for eons. Still afraid of what my arms might say or do, I resolved to wear the jacket and sizzle until the day's end. Just then, another Methodist opened the main door and new hot air rushed into the building.

My meltdown began.

With a crazed look on my face, I turned to Mimi and whispered loudly, "I can't take it anymore. It is hot! Do you hear me? It is hot – 107 degrees worth of hot. I don't like being hot and I will no longer allow my erratic upper arms to govern me. I am 45 years old. I went to college. I drive a car. I run a business. I have been married. I have survived tough times. So why am I having an upper-arm breakdown? I have a right to be cool and if people are lining up just to watch my upper arms wiggle, then let them watch! My skin was practically ready to ignite and I could bear the heat no longer."

Far smarter than I, Mimi had already discarded her jacket, revealing her upper arms to any Methodist that cared to examine them. She simply smiled as I continued my heat-related ranting.

"Besides, my Bible tells me I am made in the image of God and that includes my quivering upper arms. I don't like the way they look or the way they wobble, but from this point forward, I am going to be cool. Do you hear me? Cool! I am renouncing this jacket and hereby liberating my upper arms. I will display them openly and without shame. They are part of me and will no longer be shackled in disgrace. God loves me and God loves my upper arms. If others do not, then so be it. I am forty-five years old, I am confident, and I am made in the image of God. Attention, all United Methodists – take a look at my beloved upper arms."

⧗⧗⧗⧗⧗⧗⧗

And that, my friends, is that. I emancipated my quivering upper arms in the heat of a June day in Augusta, Georgia. That was over one year ago and I have not looked back nor have I ever regretted my decision. The only thing I do regret is the amount of time I spent hiding a part of me because I feared laughter and rejection.

We humans are quite funny and can go a little crazy over silly things. Jiggling upper arms can be embarrassing, of course. But if I really want to worry about something, it should be the hungry, the homeless, those plagued by disease, and living in a world without peace. Today there are many who desperately need everything from heart transplants to love and acceptance. Many are praying for money to pay monthly bills while others face the pain of broken families and relationships. Others are without Christ and seek meaning for their lives.

When I consider these things, I am embarrassed at the time and torment misspent on a pair of wiggling upper arms.

So I am on my way to Wal-Mart where I will ask an associate to point me to the tank tops. Plus size. And I want one in every color.

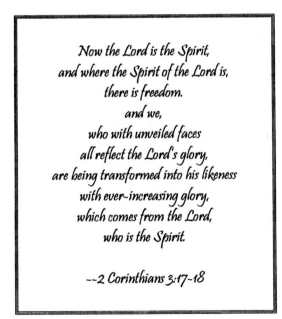

Now the Lord is the Spirit,
and where the Spirit of the Lord is,
there is freedom.
and we,
who with unveiled faces
all reflect the Lord's glory,
are being transformed into his likeness
with ever-increasing glory,
which comes from the Lord,
who is the Spirit.

--2 Corinthians 3:17-18

You know you are aging when . . .

. . .you are mugged
and
are more concerned with
rescuing your pill box
than your
credit cards!

Too Sweet For My Own Good

My lifelong battle with doctor phobia is legendary in these parts. The simple act of parking near a doctor's office raises my blood pressure twenty points – both the systolic and diastolic numbers. Days before a routine appointment I experience anxiety, heartburn, nightmares, stomach ailments, and a racing heart. Panic attacks occur on the hour. Oh, and I can also be a bit cranky.

But I go, because I realize the importance of an annual wellness exam.

I know the routine. Sign in at the front desk. Update insurance forms and personal information. Wait. Have blood work drawn. Wait. Place my arm in a blood pressure cuff. Pee in a cup. Wait. Hold completely still for the mammogram. Wait. Slide into the stirrups. Turn red with embarrassment. Wait for a final talk with the doctor so that he can tell me that everything is just fine. Things have always been fine.

But not this year.

Diagnosis: Diabetes. I have a pooped-out pancreas, resulting in too much sugar in my blood. This is a chronic disease that requires medication, changes in diet and lifestyle, stress reduction, and daily monitoring of blood sugar levels. I also have blood work drawn only a quarterly basis so my doctor can keep track of the effect diabetes is having on my body.

Diabetes. I have heard the word for years and even contemplated how horrible it must be. But diabetes was not just a word any longer. It was a diagnosis. My diagnosis. And I did not like it one bit. I took the news well, but was still skeptical. I had not experienced any of the typical symptoms of diabetes.

77

"Have you been excessively thirsty?" my doctor quizzed.
"No."
Do you spend a lot of time looking for restrooms or do you get up during the night to go?"
"No."
"Any blurred vision?"
"Not with my new progressive lenses." I proudly responded.
"What about fatigue or irritability?"
"Wait – do you mean those are symptoms of diabetes? I just thought that was part aging, working too hard, and my unique personality!"

I had not exhibited the classic symptoms, but that did not matter. The fact was that I did, indeed, have diabetes. Now I had to deal with it.

I never panicked over my unwelcome news. Instead, I began educating myself. I attended Diabetic Education classes. I subscribed to magazines, read books, searched the Internet, and talked with others who share my diagnosis – and I was shocked and astounded to learn just how many people are living with diabetes.

My ailment was an undeniably reality. A glucometer enabled me to monitor my blood sugar levels throughout the day. I began to talk about things such as glucose, test strips, endocrinology, insulin, and the pancreas. I studied potential side effects, serious complications including cardiovascular disease, kidney disease, eye problems, and trouble with the nervous system. My education produced a healthy dose of fear as I heard about strokes, heart attacks, and amputations. I began to suffer from brain-overload.

To regain perspective, I once asked a specialist, "Does anybody with diabetes ever die of old age?"

"Yes," he assured me. "If controlled, you can live a long, productive life."

Whew, I needed to hear that!

So I am now living with Type 2 Diabetes. Also known as Adult Onset Diabetes, this disease is caused by a combination of genetics, diet, stress, and lifestyle. The pancreas produces very little insulin, the hormone required to regulate blood glucose levels. Eventually, the pancreas may not be able to produce any insulin at all. Thus, the body must receive insulin through injections, pumps, or medications.

I am very lucky! A pill controls my problem and I have no need of shots or pumps. I have lost thirty pounds. I am learning more about nutrition and ways to reduce stress in my life. I now monitor cholesterol and triglyceride levels. Yes, I have diabetes, but I am now healthier than I was before my diagnosis.

Prior to seeing my doctor each quarter, I visit Judy Wallace and Emma Massey at the local lab. These ladies are two of the great treasures I have discovered in the midst of this illness – definitely a touch of *silver in the slop*. Even while having blood drawn, my medical phobia never raises its ugly head. I have Judy and Emma to thank for that. These are wonderfully compassionate women who recognize my quirks and fears. They also realize that I have strong opinions regarding certain medical procedures. For instance, I will not allow anyone to poke my arm and dig for an obscure vein. I am a weenie who will only allow blood to be drawn through a butterfly needle inserted into the top of my hand. It takes a little longer, but Judy and Emma work with me because I have shared my anxieties with them. They talk to me as a friend while doing their job. We discuss their families, the state of the world, or my latest adventures. Before I realize it, blood has been drawn and I am on my way – and it didn't even hurt. Cross my heart!

If you need a refresher course on how to treat people kindly, you need to watch Judy and Emma in action. I salute them for their compassion, understanding, and the lessons they have taught me. I tell them quite often that they are my two favorite "bloodsuckers" in the whole world!

So now I am, literally, too sweet for my own good! With additional weight loss I may reach the point at which I can control my diabetes with no medication at all. That is my goal.

Meanwhile, I continue to read, study, and educate myself. The only thing I would like better is to educate others.

Over one million people will develop diabetes this year, many of whom will remain undiagnosed, allowing their blood sugar levels to rise to dangerous levels.

Consider the symptoms. Have you experienced severe thirst, frequent urination, extreme fatigue, blurred vision, or irritability? Maybe tremendous hunger or severe weight loss? Do not let the fear of what you might find out keep you from asking your doctor to check you for diabetes. Request a Hemoglobin A1C test, a procedure that determines your average glucose level for a ninety-day period. This simple blood test will confirm or deny the presence of diabetes.

Health care professionals will tell you that diabetes has reached epidemic proportions. It can be controlled, but only if the disease has been diagnosed. And remember this – diabetes is not the worst thing that can happen to you. You can live a full, happy life. You can adjust your routine. You can eat anything you want as long as you do so responsibly. And new medications and treatments are being developed every day.

And please, understand one very important point. To know me is to know someone who is going to screw up. Some days I do not exercise or eat responsibly. My glucose numbers are not always where they should be. It is difficult to travel and stick to a wholesome diet and schedule. Plus, there are moments when I am going to eat chocolate and, be assured, I will plow you down if you try to stop me. I try not to be too hard on myself when that happens. I humbly bewail my sin and begin again.

Diabetes is not as frightening as it seemed twenty or thirty years ago. But it is a reality that requires treatment. The best gift you can give yourself is an annual wellness exam that includes testing for diabetes. Chances are you are just fine. But if the diagnosis is positive, take care of yourself.

So give your doctor a call. And if a blood test is needed, let me know. I'll tell Judy and Emma to watch for you.

> *Are not five sparrows sold for two pennies?*
> *Yet not one of them is forgotten by God.*
> *Indeed, the very hairs of your head*
> *are numbered.*
> *Don't be afraid;*
> *you are worth more than many sparrows.*
>
> *--Luke 12:6-7*

Additional information may be obtained through:

The American Diabetes Association
1701 North Beauregard Street
Alexandria, VA 22311
1-800-Diabetes
www.diabetes.org

*For years I have heard a
vicious rumor that
once you reach forty,
your body begins to fall apart.*

*I want to address this rumor
once and for all
to set the record straight.*

OF COURSE IT DOES!

Lessons

*I am old enough
to tell the truth.
It is one of the
privileges of age.*

*--Georges Clemenceau
(1841-1929)*

"Have you heard any
juicy gossip lately?
Got any good dirt
on anybody?"

"No,
I haven't been
to church
lately."

--Portion of an actual conversation
between two teenagers.

Hey, Got Any Hershey Bars?

*C*ornbread, turnip greens, and Brunswick Stew. These southern delicacies were topics of a recent program I shared with a local civic group. However unpretentious, this cuisine is part of our shared heritage. So even though we were strangers when the night began, we spent the evening laughing and sharing our lives in the spirit of Southern hospitality. When I left I felt as though I had gained 150 new friends.

As a surprise gift, the gracious group presented me with a very generous gift certificate to a Five Star Restaurant – a place certainly not known for serving turnip greens and such. Could I make the transition from cornbread to Crème Brule? I would give it my best effort!

Because the gift certificate included funds sufficient for two meals, I asked my friend, Jennifer Huycke, to accompany me. This decision was not easy and involved some initial hesitation. Why? Because Jennifer has a unique way of embarrassing me when I am trying to pretend I am classy and refined. (Please reference *Putting on the Ritz* from my first book, *Silver in the Slop*).

I lectured her before we left for the restaurant.

"Please behave tonight," I begged. "This gift certificate has MY name on it so if you cause a scene, they will only remember my name. I know it will be difficult, but could you please, please, please try to keep things under control?"

Free food was involved so, of course, Jennifer promised. However, based on several past experiences, I remained skeptical regarding her behavior.

Jennifer's husband, the Rev. Dick Huycke, was elected babysitter for their two children and we scheduled our outing for the following Friday night. We dressed in our Sunday best and our Five Star adventure began.

Arriving at the elegant restaurant known for its French and Mediterranean cuisine, a uniformed valet quickly disappeared with my keys and my car. Jennifer and I entered the establishment boasting exquisite décor, antiques, fresh flowers, glowing candles, and overstuffed chairs at each perfectly set table. We were led to a table with a breathtaking view of the Atlanta skyline.

Once seated, the very attentive staff described their wide variety of wines. We declined and ordered iced tea instead. Our glasses arrived accompanied by crystal containers holding a clear liquid that, we were told, was melted sugar for sweetening the tea to our desired taste. Menus were presented and we were left alone for a few moments to make our dinner choices. Jennifer, I was relieved to observe, was behaving quite appropriately.

As we examined the menu, we realized how little we knew about food – even though we have been eating it all our lives. The bill of fare contained elaborate descriptions of items we did not recognize and could not pronounce. Even so, I certainly was not going to have the waiter describe each entrée to me.

"What is this stuff?" Jennifer whispered.

"I have no idea," I whispered back. "Just go for anything that has chicken in the description. Chicken is a safe bet – you can do a lot to it, but it is still chicken."

Jennifer and I also had a great advantage here. As wives of United Methodist ministers, we have had a lot of experience with chicken over the years. In fact, we have consumed the "Gospel Bird" in almost every recipe known to humankind. We have been in the trenches. We are chicken veterans.

We ordered the chicken. How it would be prepared and what would accompany it remained a mystery – even after the dish arrived. But it was delicious! We knew we were eating chicken (for free!) and enjoying a girl's night out so all seemed right with the world.

We watched the city lights and soon began to relax as we sat by a warm fireplace. We even ate the other unknown items accompanying our chicken while we drank our iced tea sweetened with liquid sugar from crystal containers. By the middle of the meal we began to feel quite cultured.

When the chicken disappeared, the server returned to discuss the dessert menu. The restaurant was famous for its captivating desserts and our waiter began a rather lengthy recitation of the delights of each sweet offering.

"We have a White Chocolate Soufflé accompanied by a delicate Belgium Ice Cream or a Cherry Soufflé complemented by a Vanilla Kirsch Cream Anglaise."

What?

He continued.

"Perhaps you would prefer our Double Chocolate Cake with Brandied Raspberry Sauce or the Fresh Fruit Torte with sweetened whipped cream topped with grated chocolate."

My head was spinning. Jennifer's cholesterol level jumped 72 points just by listening to him.

He continued.

"Many clients simply rave about our Almond Tart served with fresh blueberries and drizzled with a delightful Grand Marnier Sauce."

I was slipping into a diabetic coma.

He continued.

"A particular favorite of mine is the Cream Cheese Torte baked with just a hint of cinnamon and covered with a rich toffee syrup that is to die for!"

The monologue seemed endless. I never knew there were so many soufflés and glazes and sauces on the planet. Dessert was no longer fun. It had suddenly become very complicated.

Jennifer obviously shared my sentiments and could take no more. Despite my earlier lecture, in her best Southern drawl she suddenly blurted, "Hey, got any Hershey Bars?"

Staring at her with wide eyes and shocked expression, our waiter grabbed his chest right in the middle of our very exclusive Five Star Restaurant. I laughed out loud and toasted Jennifer with my glass of iced tea sweetened with liquid sugar.

Life in this world-class restaurant seemed quite complex for two ordinary people like Jennifer and me. And I suddenly began to crave a Hershey Bar myself – plain milk chocolate in a simple brown wrapper.

While the waiter clutched his chest and turned an odd shade of gray, Jennifer and I bid farewell to the very nice restaurant. We completely bypassed the fancy desserts and bought Hershey Bars for each of us at an Amoco Station on the way home. We even purchased Hershey Bars for Dick and their two children. No sauces, no syrups, no drizzles, no Grand Marnier. With extreme delight, we feasted on our plain milk chocolate treats swathed in a simple brown wrapper.

Why do we allow simple things to become so complicated? We do this in our daily lives, we do this in schools, we do this in our relationships. And we do it in our churches. Even as Christians with the best of intentions, we can become completely bogged down with doctrine, denominations, and semantics. We debate theology, homiletics, and church polity. We create disputes over discipline, situational ethics, and the definition of right and wrong. We allow minor details to mushroom into major issues. Churches split. Wars have been fought, lives lost, and relationships destroyed in the name of God and religion.

We humans are a humorous lot. We easily get caught up in the sauces and syrups of complicated details when God just wants us to love one another – a decree as simple as a Hershey Bar in a world of soufflés.

"A new command I give to you: Love one another. As I have loved you, so you must love one another. By this all men

will know you are my disciples, if you love one another" (John 13:34-35).

Seems pretty straightforward, don't you think? Why don't we discuss it over a Hershey Bar?

> *The law of the Lord is perfect,*
> *reviving the soul,*
> *The statutes of the Lord are trustworthy,*
> *making wise the simple.*
>
> *-- Psalm 19:7*

Noticing his father's
receding hairline
one morning,
Wesley Shelnutt said to
his father and my friend,
the Rev. Dr. Dee Shelnutt,
"Wow, Dad,
you have a
lot more face to wash
than you used to."

-- Wesley Shelnutt, Age 13

A True Education = Life Lessons

*C*ollege is a true rite of passage and a step into adulthood. I had always dreamed of going to college even though no one else in my family had ever pursued higher education. From my earliest memory, I had heard of LaGrange College, less than an hour south of my hometown of Newnan, Georgia. So I made my decision to attend this United Methodist College long before I graduated from Newnan High School. I also made the decision knowing full well that there were no financial resources within my family for me to attend LaGrange or any other college.

But God makes a way when there is no way.

Thus, I am now a graduate of LaGrange College and eternally grateful for the four years I studied, worked, worshipped, laughed and lived on campus. I received an outstanding education and was even one of those disgusting students who made all A's, except for one B in Creative Writing! My education, however, was far more than academic. The "life lessons" I learned at LaGrange College have served me far better than the traditional curriculum of reading, writing, and 'rithmetic.

I am thankful for the educators who continue to impact my life more than 20 years (how did it get to be 20 years?) after graduation. No doubt, I could write a book about my four years at LaGrange College. However, for the sake of time and space, consider the following individuals who are representative of many other excellent educators. They are confirmation that our colleges and universities are in very capable hands.

91

❖ Dr. Frank McCook, Professor of Religion, had a reputation as a no-nonsense professor whose classes were intense and difficult. I have no doubt that he rather enjoyed this reputation. Yet each year he invited his students into his home where he shared homemade ice cream (peppermint was our favorite) and provided us the chance to know him – and one another – on a more personal level.

This professor who frightened me many years ago just e-mailed me last week to simply ask how I was doing. He is proof that a good teacher remembers students long after the classes are over and the diplomas are awarded.

Frank McCook showed me that a professor may be tough to bring out the best in a student and that underneath a gruff exterior often beats a heart of gold.

❖ Dr. David Naglee, Professor of Religion, bravely entered the "Miss LaGrange College" Male Beauty Pageant as the representative of our Wesley Fellowship group one year. This distinguished and learned man dressed in a flowing white dress filled with two strategically placed balloons to emulate a bountiful chest. With eye shadow and bright red lipstick, he sashayed amid a gym filled with his students and colleagues.

For the talent competition, he carefully placed a saw between his knees and played music using a violin bow pulled against the unusual instrument. A silent audience gazed in amazement as beautiful music filled the gymnasium. (Personally, I was praying that he would not pull the bow too quickly and accidentally puncture his "chest" during the competition.)

Dr. Naglee stole the show and won first place that evening. David Naglee showed me that, regardless of the many awards and degrees listed on your resume, you should never take yourself too seriously. He was exuberant and joyous and, by example, taught me that having fun is not a frivolous luxury, but one of the basic necessities of life.

❖ Ann Bailey, Professor of Spanish, invited me to take part in a travel/study seminar to Mexico in 1977. Knowing I had no financial resources for such a trip, Mrs. Bailey paid my way so that I could be a part of this event.

Amid my emotional protests, she quietly said something I have never forgotten: "Cathy, the worst thing you can do is to refuse a gift someone wants to give you."

She taught me Spanish language and literature, but Ann Bailey also taught me to receive. Though sometimes difficult, being a gracious receiver is important. Regardless of pride and embarrassment, there are times I should simply smile and genuinely say, "Thank You!"

❖ Dr. Robert Preston Price, Ordained United Methodist Minister and Professor of Psychology, was a teacher, friend and a mentor. For 3 ½ years I served as student assistant to Dr. Price and the Department of Psychology as part of my College Work-Study program. I answered the phone, took phone messages, typed letters, and performed general office work while getting to know this wonderful man.

"Expect spiritual surprises," he often told me, "the small things around you that show God is at work." I took his advice and began looking for God in all things and I found God to be ever-present.

Just before graduation, Dr. Price presented me with $1,000 gift to use toward earning my Master's Degree in Christian Education at Scarritt College in Nashville, Tennessee. Dr. Price had faith in me as evidenced through his time, his lessons, and his generosity. If Dr. Robert Preston Price saw potential and had faith in me, I should certainly have faith in myself. I still look for those "spiritual surprises" and many are the basis for the stories that fill my books.

The words of St. Francis of Assisi again challenge us: *"Always be a witness for Christ – if necessary, use words."*
While these men and women used words, their greatest textbooks were the lives they led.

Perfection is present neither in our schools or our churches. But goodness is extraordinarily present. It is with a grateful heart that I recall the life lessons that made me a better student but, more importantly, a better human being.

With love and gratitude,
Cathy Lee Phillips
Class of '78

Choose my instruction instead of silver,
knowledge rather than choice gold,
for wisdom is more precious than rubies,
and nothing you desire can compare with her.

--Proverbs 8:10-11

Shhh . . . Jesus is in the Room

Six first-grade teachers at Garrett Elementary School held their breaths and glanced nervously about the room. They were receiving the list of children they would educate, guide, and discipline for the coming school year. They were friends and colleagues who wished no hardship on anyone, but each secretly prayed, "Please, Lord, give him to another teacher."

After taking kindergarten by storm, Jason Montgomery was entering the first grade. In his wake, he left behind one distraught kindergarten teacher (still in therapy), one troubled paraprofessional (who underwent a voluntary hysterectomy over the summer), and one weary principal who knew the child and his parents on a first-name basis. He also had all their phone numbers committed to memory. Jason Montgomery was talkative, hyperactive, and an ingenious troublemaker. He defied adults, intimidated classmates, and cast fear into the hearts of those teachers who waited anxiously to learn which of them would be Jason Montgomery's next target. The sheets were distributed and, almost immediately, a dreadful wail arose from the back left corner of the room. Mrs. Donovan, a seasoned veteran who had taught first grade for well over a decade, appeared catatonic, her student list clenched tightly in her right hand.

The principal broke the silence.

"Don't worry, Mrs. Donovan, your therapy will be covered by our Worker's Comp Insurance."

The family of teachers at Garrett Elementary School gathered around to offer support, but Mrs. Donovan took a deep breath and vowed not to be driven to despair by Jason Montgomery, Child Terrorist. For the next three days, she concentrated on decorating and preparing her classroom for the onslaught of students who would soon be arriving. Her final chore was to place a name board on the wall – a big blue poster listing the name of every child in her class.

A varied collection of first-graders and parents entered her room the next morning and Mrs. Donovan greeted all with her typical smile. She trembled slightly when she spotted Jason Montgomery accompanied by his mother. Looking somewhat battered and fatigued, Mrs. Montgomery seemed practically joyful when she left her son in the capable hands of his new teacher. She returned to her car and prayed for Jason's conduct and Mrs. Donovan's nerves. Relishing the golden silence inside the car, she drove home, wondering just how soon it would be before the principal would call with details of Jason's latest disruption.

Meanwhile, Mrs. Donovan greeted her students.

"I want to learn your names so I have made name tags for each of you to wear today. Please sit very still while I place the name tag on your shirt."

Everyone, including Jason Montgomery, obeyed.

Then Mrs. Donovan pointed to the big blue poster on the wall.

"Boys and girls, this is a list of all your new friends. While I learn your names, I want you to learn the names of all the other boys and girls in our class."

The name of every student was listed in alphabetical order on the big blue name board.

Mrs. Donovan then talked about school rules, read a book, and taught her students a new song, all the while keeping Jason Montgomery under constant surveillance. But Jason never caused a problem. To her surprise, he never talked out of turn, wandered around the room, or insulted the other students.

Was this the real Jason Montgomery? The teacher could not comprehend Jason's behavior. Neither did the principal. Neither did the other first-grade teachers who took turns checking on Mrs. Donovan throughout the day. And neither did Mrs. Montgomery when she picked Jason up at the end of the day.

"Jason was a good boy?" his mother asked suspiciously.

"A perfect angel."

Although Mrs. Montgomery praised Jason for his astonishing behavior, she was certain it would not continue.

But it did continue – through the first week, the first month, and the first six weeks of the school year. There were no phone calls from a frantic principal and no notes from a beleaguered teacher. Unbelievable!

As the seventh week began, Mrs. Donovan called Mrs. Montgomery for a parent-teacher conference.

"Please bring Jason along," Mrs. Donovan requested.

"I knew it would not last," Jason's mother thought. "Here comes the bad news."

Not so. Mrs. Donovan simply wanted to praise and congratulate Jason in the presence of his mother.

Astounded, Jason's mother could no longer keep quiet. Leaning toward her son, she asked, "Honey, you have been such a good boy this year and I am very proud of you. But why have you been so good this year when you were always in trouble last year?"

Jason raised his blue eyes and simply said, "Jesus is in my room."

"Yes, Jason, we believe Jesus is everywhere, but . . ."

"But, Mommy, Jesus really is in my room. Look!"

Jason pointed to the big blue name board that alphabetically listed the students in Mrs. Donovan's class.

Garrett Elementary School had a variety of students, many of whom were Hispanic, including Jesus Alvarez who was listed first on the big blue name board. Though Jason had not learned a lot of words, he certainly recognized the name of JESUS when he saw it.

97

Jason's mother and teacher could barely contain their laughter.

"Oh, Jason, let me explain. You see . . ."

Clearing her throat and interrupting, the wise first-grade teacher spoke, "Mrs. Montgomery, we really do not need to confuse Jason with a lot of unnecessary details, do we?" Mrs. Donovan obviously knew a good thing when she saw one.

"You are right, Mrs. Donovan. Thank you. I just hope Jason will always have Jesus in his room."

"Amen to that," his teacher smiled. "Amen to that."

What about you? Been misbehaving?

You had better straighten up and be on your best behavior. Admit it – Jesus is in the room.

Where can I go from your Spirit?
Where can I flee from your presence?
If I go up to the heavens, you are there;
If I make my bed in the depths, you are there.
If I rise on the wings of the dawn,
If I settle on the far side of the sea,
Even then your hand will guide me,
Your right hand will hold me fast.

--Psalm 139:7-10

Musings from Glacier Bay

Glacier Bay, Alaska.

My eyes moved quickly in every direction. I wanted to view everything, every brilliant image of that majestic place. Speechless, I gazed at the most awesome sights I had ever seen. The frozen beauty was overwhelming. Snow-capped mountains rose in the distance like soaring skyscrapers. The warm color of autumn leaves decorated the trees growing on the mountainsides. Their reds and yellows were a colorful contrast to the icy whites and blues of the glaciers surrounding our mammoth ship. Playful puffins romped on the edge of vast sheets of ice while gray seals slid in and out of the frigid water like greased pigs at a county fair. I grew colder just watching their sub-zero festivities.

Craggy glaciers were everywhere – mammoth sheets of ice, air, water, and sediment that had inched toward the water's edge at leisurely speeds over hundreds of years. Their weathered edges possessed a distinctive beauty in shades of blues and browns. Hundreds of icebergs floated in the frigid water beneath the Regal Princess cruise liner. From our vantage point high above the water, they look minuscule. Yet everyone knows that these enormous chunks of ice have the potential to sink unsinkable ships.

Alaska fascinates me and I have always dreamed of seeing this mind-boggling scenery. I can scarcely believe I am standing amid this beauty, but bitterly cold temperatures remind me that I am in Alaska in late September. Through four layers of clothing, I shiver in the freezing temperatures. Still, I give no thought to retreating to the cabin. There is simply too much of God in this place and I refuse to miss a single moment of the wonder of it all.

An awesome quiet pervades Glacier Bay, a silence occasionally interrupted by the thunderous roar of huge sections of ice splintering from the glacier's edge and crashing into the sea. This process, known as calving, is part of the natural order of this place. While they may seem stationary, glaciers are actually moving objects, even though their progress is unbelievably slow – perhaps only a few feet each year. Their movement forms small fissures that eventually mature into large cracks as the glacier slowly advances toward the sea. The rifts widen and the weight of the ice finally causes large sections to break away from the glacier. The ice calves and tumbles into the cold water below. Thus, an iceberg – jagged, immense, and dangerous – is formed.

For several hours I stand on the deck with my friend, Phyllis. We have remained friends since high school and have long talked of cruising to Alaska, principally to see Glacier Bay. We talk for a while and then retreat into our own thoughts.

My husband, Jerry, died a few months prior to this trip. How I wish he could have been standing beside me, sharing the majesty of Glacier Bay. I began to long for him and could feel the cold fingers of grief claw at my emotions.

Just then I again heard the deep rumble of calving ice. I turned precisely at the moment an immense portion of ice tore away from a glacier and plummeted into the sea. Small pieces of ice flew in various directions as it fell, almost as though it were coming apart. Upon impact, shock waves skipped across the water. The iceberg dipped and bobbed as though it could not decide which way was up. Soon the waves subsided and the bulky, cumbersome iceberg began to position itself. Once the shock subsided, the iceberg sat upright, the bulk of it resting far beneath the surface. The mass began to float as the current towed it further and further away from the glacier. Things had just changed dramatically and forever for that iceberg. Once a part of something greater than itself, it now floated alone in the cold and icy water of Glacier Bay, Alaska.

⧗⧗⧗⧗⧗⧗⧗

I wanted to name that iceberg "Cathy" because I felt so akin to it and could easily identify with what it had just experienced.

While married to Jerry, I, too, was part of something greater than myself. What a wonderful gift it was to share my life with a man who loved and supported me, regardless of my inadequacies, faults, and warts. Jerry and I embraced one another just as surely as the glacier once embraced the iceberg. They had been together for so long that, no doubt, the iceberg felt it would forever remain a part of the massive glacier. And while I do realize I am personalizing an inanimate object, I would assume that, before calving, the ice fit perfectly against the glacier. In my mind, this ice was comfortable, content, and satisfied. If there were a choice to be made, no doubt this iceberg named "Cathy" would have happily remained forever with the glacier.

But staying in one place is not the nature of glaciers or icebergs . . . or even human beings. Sometimes small fissures enter our lives – such as Jerry's illness – and before we know what is happening, large cracks develop that threaten our existence. And one day, when we are simply living our lives, a horrifying occurrence changes us completely and for all time. We feel as though we might fall apart while tumbling into the cold unknown. Shock stuns and dazes us. We struggle to get our bearings, upright ourselves, and make peace with our new way of life. This takes time. The amount of time varies with each person. In fear and distress, we try to understand how life can change so completely in a moment's time.

The iceberg named "Cathy" reminded me of how I felt following Jerry's death – ripped away from something safe and wonderful, then struggling in cold, unfamiliar territory. The current of life moved me because there were tasks that had to be completed. Though I met all my basic responsibilities, I was too stunned to do little else. I floated through life, feeling that each passing moment only pulled me further away from the man and the life I had loved.

I remained on deck until our ship departed Glacier Bay that September evening. Until the last moment, I watched the mountains, ice, and glaciers. I tried to commit every bit of the overwhelming beauty to memory so that I could bring it to mind on days when I experience grief or the stress of everyday life.

And the iceberg named "Cathy?" By the time our ship departed, it had drifted a good distance from the glacier. It had taken time, but the iceberg was no longer dipping and diving in the water. The shock waves were gone and the water beneath it was cold but calm. Puffins were already populating the jagged edges and gray seals slid onto the ice with great ease. The iceberg was no longer part of the glacier, but it was strong, upright, and moving forward with a new life of its own.

There are times when I imagine the iceberg named "Cathy" looks back with longing to the life it once shared with the glacier. That is perfectly natural. Still, I trust the iceberg has adjusted to the change, has made friends with the puffins and the seals, and has made peace with its new, unique place in the beauty of God's creation.

Oh, just in case you are wondering, the person named "Cathy" has done the same.

> *He reached down from on high and took hold of me;*
> *He drew me out of deep waters.*
>
> *-- Psalm 18:16*

Perspective

In youth
we learn,
in old age
we understand.

-- Marie von Ebner-Eschenbach
(1830-1916)

My friend,
Lynne Murphy,
is having a colonoscopy next week
and she is actually
looking forward to it.

Why?

In her words:
"This will be the most intimacy
I've experienced
in 10 years."

Bad Attitude? Pay Up!

*F*rom the moment I first met Susan, it was obvious that she loved Duncan. Her face would light up when she spoke of him. Duncan was just about perfect, Susan believed – handsome, friendly, loving, and the ideal companion.

"I wish I could find a man like that," I stated, unable to hide my envy.

"A man?" Susan laughed. "No, Cathy, Duncan is my dog!"

(This fact does not dissuade me from still wanting to meet a man who is handsome, friendly, loving, and the ideal companion.)

I love dogs. In fact, I had a dog at the time – an English Springer Spaniel just like Duncan, so I knew how happy and loyal this breed could be. I looked forward to meeting Duncan as I drove to Susan's home one Monday night for a meeting of United Methodist Women. Entering her home, I looked for this loving, perfect dog.

That is when Duncan growled and went for my throat.

"So this is your sweet Duncan," I said, tightly pressing a cloth against the blood pouring from the open wounds decorating my neck. Duncan greeted other guests in a similar fashion and Susan, ever the gracious hostess, passed around a large box of bandages before locking Duncan in her bedroom.

"Did you use a dead bolt?" I inquired with a shaky voice.

While Duncan was obviously the perfect companion for Susan, I was clearly convinced than his trainer had been none other than Satan himself.

Several months later I was invited to spend a week with Susan and her family at their beach home on Pawley's Island, South Carolina. Though I did not want to seem ungrateful, for my personal safety I felt it necessary to ask the obvious question: "Will Demon Doggie be there?"

I wanted to know whether to purchase a suit of armor I had been eyeing since first meeting Duncan.

Duncan did go to the beach, but I made sure some large piece of furniture was always between us. On the third night, though, Duncan actually began to warm up to me. In fact, as we all talked on the porch that hot summer night, the creature actually approached me without bearing his teeth. Before long he sat beside me and, though tentatively at first, I began to pet him. Each person, me included, held his or her breath as Duncan lay very still beside me until bedtime. Had I actually bonded with the Demon Doggie? What a conquest! What a triumph! I felt invincible!

The next night Duncan growled and went for my throat.

I felt like a complete failure until Susan admitted that I was not the only one on Duncan's hit list. In fact, she had taken Demon Doggie for his summer coiffure just a few days earlier. Leaving Duncan in the capable hands of an experienced groomer, Susan returned later in the day to retrieve her beloved dog. She was quite surprised when the groomer himself met her personally at the front desk. She was even more surprised when he presented her with a bill that was $25 higher than the amount originally quoted.

"Why was I charged an extra $25?" Susan inquired.

The groomer advised Susan that Duncan had been a most difficult client. The dog had growled, snapped, and generally scared the dickens out of anyone who approached him. Thus, they had assessed Duncan with a $25 "Bad Attitude Fee."

I laughed out loud. "A Bad Attitude Fee? I am surprised they stopped at a mere $25!"

There is no warm and fuzzy ending to this story. I never won Duncan's friendship. While he loves Susan unquestionably, he still growls and goes for my throat. Therefore, I respect his teeth and his bad attitude and maintain a safe distance. And it gives me some comfort to know I am not the only person who refers to him as "Demon Doggie."

But I have learned something from Duncan.

A bad attitude makes everyone miserable. And if I were charged $25 each time I had a bad attitude, I would be literally on the front step of the poor house. Yet I suffer from a bad attitude far more often than I should.

Therefore, in Duncan's honor, I have begun something new. I now have a "Bad Attitude Jar" on my desk and I have vowed to place one dollar into it every time I cop a bad attitude. Yes, I know Duncan was charged $25 for his fee, but let's be reasonable – I am simply not rich enough to give up $25 each time I sulk or bellyache. But perhaps this form of behavior modification will help me nonetheless.

There are many circumstances over which I have no control. However, I can control my response to these circumstances. For instance, will I be grateful for my countless blessings or whine and pout about what I do not have? Will I face difficult days with anger and depression or will I hold my head high and allow God's presence to guide me? Will I become obsessed with handling everything myself or will I slow down, take a deep breath, and pray for direction? Will I enjoy the peace that passes all understanding or live with fear and anxiety? Will I be consumed with envy and jealousy or gratefully acknowledge all God has given me? Will I face each day with dread or confidently face the future with God as my deliverer? Will I seek to be happy and enjoy my life or go for someone's throat when things do not go my way? Will I laugh often and try not to take myself too seriously?

I pray that my Bad Attitude Jar is not filled and overflowing at the end of the year.

Help me control my attitude, Dear Lord. And when I feel things are going too rough, remind me of Duncan the Demon Doggie who has now alienated every groomer in the metro Atlanta area. Thus, Susan herself now clips and grooms Duncan and, in her own words, Duncan sports the "most hideous" haircut of any dog she knows.

Forgive my bad attitude, Lord, but knowing that Duncan has a bad hair day -- every day -- makes me feel a lot better!

You were taught,
with regard to your former way of life,
to put off your old self,
which is being corrupted by its deceitful desires;
to be made new in the attitude of your minds;
and to put on the new self,
created to be like God
in true righteousness and holiness.

--Ephesians 4:22-24

Some Days Are a Drag - No Bull!

hough he had more legs, stomachs, and horns than the average Posey Road resident, Beetlebomm the bull had one thing in common with the rest of us – he did not like Raylinda Dupree.

My cousin twice-removed on my Mama's side, Raylinda was the scourge of my childhood. When her parents divorced, she came to live with us and I, only two years her senior, was appointed her "protector." This was no easy task. Raylinda possessed a vicious tongue, wicked arrogance, and a mean spirit that could enrage the most benevolent adult. I have learned that some people are just that way.

"I'd rather spend my day with a pole cat than that girl," said our neighbor, Mr. Wright.

Beetlebomm obviously shared Mr. Wright's point of view.

Weighing about 1200 pounds with two large, menacing horns, Beetlebomm was as well known on Posey Road as Raylinda – but far more popular! Despite his ominous looks, he was a gentle giant. His huge black eyes relayed a sincere *thank you* when I fed him sugar cubes and apples, his rough tongue sliding across my open palm. I was a tomboy at that age and very fond of all the animals on our farm, but Beetlebomm was my favorite by far. So it was only natural that I would occasionally take a walk with my friend. In fact, Beetlebomm and I would often stroll up and down Posey Road. With only a rope around his neck, Beetlebomm walked slowly, surveying his territory and greeting neighbors eager to offer him attention or a tasty treat. The rope was really unnecessary because, loving the attention, the bull never tried to run. Besides, I was only ten years old and, had he decided to dart, I could never have stopped him.

In short, Beetlebomm was "King of the Farm" and loved everyone. Everyone except, Raylinda Dupree, of course. He treated her with an indifference that bordered on disdain, which I believe demonstrated an impressive degree of animal instinct. But it made Raylinda more determined than ever to win his affection. She offered treats, but he snorted and chose to eat grass instead. When she persisted, Beetlebomm flicked his tail sharply in her direction. Raylinda responded with a stomp of her foot, a string of harsh words, and a swat in his direction. Beetlebomm would then lower his head and proudly display his long horns until Raylinda ran away.

Gotta love that bull!

Things finally changed one memorable October morning. Beetlebomm stood completely still as I slipped the rope over his horns and neck. Leaving the pasture, we turned onto Posey Road and walked only a short distance before Raylinda jumped in front of us. Startled by this sudden, and unwelcome, intrusion, Beetlebomm uttered a low growl.

"Give me the rope," Raylinda demanded.

Beetlebomm shook his head sharply. Raylinda grabbed the rope, startling the bull and causing him to take a few agitated steps.

I begged Raylinda to back away, but she stood firm. I began to worry because, though Beetlebomm was gentle and friendly, he was still a 1200-pound bull with long horns and a definite dislike of Raylinda Dupree. I tried to explain these facts to the scourge of my childhood, but Raylinda, as usual, was only interested in getting what she wanted.

Jerking the rope from my hands, Raylinda gave me a haughty look. That is the last glimpse I had of her before Beetlebomm began to run. Down Posey Road, through the remains of the summer garden, across a ditch filled with muddy water, and past the muscadines, Beetlebomm raced around the farm as Raylinda, flopping this way and that, dangled from the rope around his neck. They passed the smoke house, the pink dogwood tree, and beneath a load of towels Mama had just hung on the clothesline.

Raylinda screamed but Beetlebomm showed no signs of slowing his pace. Realizing the bull was quite agitated and would probably keep running "until the cows came home," I yelled to Raylinda, "Let go of the rope!"

This was the obvious solution to her rather precarious situation. I yelled again and again but Raylinda paid no attention to me. She held tightly to the rope even as Beetlebomm ran toward the apple trees and the cow pasture filled with . . . well . . . . fertilizer.

"Let go of the rope, Raylinda!"

Maybe it was because she thought the bull would finally stop. Maybe it was because she was afraid. Maybe it was because she was plain hardheaded. Maybe it was because she panicked and was unable to think, but it seemed an eternity before Raylinda let go of the rope and the itinerant bull. Though scratched and bruised, she immediately jumped to her feet, screaming spirited insults and hurling rocks at Beetlebomm. The bull ran into the woods and it was late evening before he appeared at our house again. And maybe I just imagined it, but I could have sworn there was a smile on his face.

In my mind I can still see Raylinda bouncing behind a 1200-pound runaway bull that had obviously reached the end of his rope. And I will admit that the image still makes me smile on occasion. Though she really brought this on herself, Raylinda remained angry at that bull until the day he died. Yet it was Raylinda who refused to let go of the rope and, as a result, was yanked and tugged behind one seriously aggravated bull.

So what is the point of my meandering, you ask? Well, some days it makes me giggle. But I also learned a rather simple lesson straight from Posey Road and Raylinda Dupree.

When a bunch of bull is dragging you down, there comes a time when you should simply LET IT GO!

> *Flee the evil desires of youth,*
> *and pursue righteousness,*
> *faith, love and peace,*
> *along with those who call on the Lord*
> *out of a pure heart.*
>
> *--2 Timothy 2:22*

Life's Great Lies

(The age 46 Version –
Subject to change without notice)

1. Life is fair.
2. One size fits all.
3. All families resemble a Norman Rockwell painting.
4. The check is in the mail.
5. If you experience a tough time, it is because you have sinned and God is punishing you.
6. Mother knows best.
7. Father knows best.
8. This will only hurt a little bit.
9. Try the brussel sprouts – you'll like them.
10. Call me if there is anything I can do.
11. You will never be able to do that.
12. If you do your best, be kind to others, and follow the 10 Commandments, life will treat you well.
13. You should not cry.
14. Your family will always love you.
15. This will only take five minutes.
16. Children always outlive their parents.
17. Ministers are holy, kind and perfect.
18. If you cross your eyes, they will get stuck that way.
19. Oh, that will never happen to me!
20. This is nothing to be upset about.

*After years of
buying and wearing clothes,
I have discovered
one indisputable fact --*

*Elastic
Is
My
Friend!*

Ray's Eagles

*D*usk was gently settling upon the mountain home of my friends Ray and Virginia Cox, suggesting it was time for me to leave their pleasant company and make my way home.

Virginia Cox first greeted me in 1961 when I entered Madras School (Madras, Georgia, is a booming metropolis just outside of Newnan) and her first grade classroom. I loved this teacher who taught me to read, write, and color between the lines. Except for one unfortunate incident when I was banished to stand in a corner, my first grade memories were happy ones.

Regarding the aforementioned "corner standing incident," I will admit that Mrs. Cox did see me slug Jimmy Jackson. However, she was unaware that he had just kissed me and I was merely defending my first grade honor.

When the school year ended, I raced from the classroom, anxious to begin my summer vacation. I did not know that Mrs. Cox had been reassigned to a different school and I would not see her when the Madras School doors opened in the fall. In fact, I would not see her for a very long time.

So it was with great surprise that just a few years ago, I received a letter from my first grade teacher. She had read my first book and tracked me down through mutual friends. We talked on the phone, laughing about some of those memories of '62, and then made a date for lunch, wondering if we would recognize one another.

"I remember you as a short, chubby, brown-eyed girl, always grinning, with a pixie haircut," Mrs. Cox laughed.

"Same description plus 40 years," I told her.

We recognized one another quite easily and have enjoyed our renewed acquaintance since then. As we talked one day, she said, "Cathy, don't you think it is about time you called me *Virginia*?"

I was astounded. I was honored. I felt as though I was breaking a cardinal rule of Madras School etiquette. But as our friendship grew, her first name began to roll off my tongue quite naturally.

This renewed friendship with Virginia has been a double blessing because I have also gotten to know her husband, Ray. With a quick wit and a ready smile, Ray finds pleasure in helping others through his work with the Lion's Club, the Helping Hands Ministry at the Baptist Church, and collecting items for the community Thrift Store. He visits hospitals and leaves homemade notebooks packed with jokes and funny stories cut from the pages of Reader's Digest, newspapers, and other sources.

"Sometimes humor is the best prescription of all," he firmly maintains.

Ray delights in nature. Their yard is adorned with the deep greens of trees and plants punctuated by brilliant flowers throughout the year. No bird or butterfly escapes his watchful eye and he treasures the presence of God he sees reflected in each ordinary creature.

But in the dusk of this particular day, I began to worry about Ray and Virginia.

"Before you go, you need to see Ray's eagles," Virginia mentioned.

A congregation of eagles? In Dahlonega?

Several years ago I visited Alaska where I rafted through the splendor of the Chilkat Bald Eagle Preserve, the home of hundreds of majestic bald eagles. I spent the day awestruck as I watched these beautiful creatures take to the sky over Alaska's mountains and glaciers. It was autumn in Alaska and the eagles soared high above the red, orange, and golden leaves adorning the lowlands and the mountains. Though I was shivering with cold, I was amazed at the beauty of nature surrounding me. It was easy to understand why the Bible speaks of the strength and grandeur of the eagle in some of my favorite verses. That was a day I will never forget. But this day I was a long way from Alaska and I just could not imagine an assemblage of eagles living at the Cox home in Dahlonega, Georgia.

Ray joined us on their large porch.

"Has Virginia told you about my eagles? They will be coming home soon and filling the trees just behind the house. You have to stay long enough to see them."

I began to fear that Ray had taken a tumble out of the "Reality Tree" and hit a few branches during his fall. Suddenly, though, large birds appeared overhead. They flew from every direction and settled into the tall pine trees behind Ray and Virginia's mountain home. Yes, they were birds, but certainly not eagles. Trust me. I am a country girl and I can recognize a bunch of nasty, disgusting buzzards when I see them. These were most definitely buzzards. Not hawks or even "country airplanes," a phrase Virginia's dad used to describe black Georgia crows. No, these were definitely buzzards – scavengers that feasted on road-kill and sick, weakened animals. These ugly creatures bore no resemblance to the regal eagles of Alaska and the Chilkat Bald Eagle Preserve. Furthermore, I began to feel like an unwilling participant in a Hitchcock movie as these hideous birds swarmed and roosted in the nearby trees.

"Should I dial 911?" I wondered as I watched Ray and Virginia eagerly gaze at each "eagle-wanna-be." Had this lovely couple truly lost their grip on reality?

Sensing my bewilderment, Ray explained, "These birds roost in our trees every night and I've grown accustomed to them. And, yes, I know they are buzzards."

I breathed a sigh of relief and loosened the grip on my cell phone.

"But while they are here, I like to think of them as my eagles instead of ugly old buzzards," Ray said with a smile and a twinkle in his eyes.

I was quite relieved to learn that neither Ray nor Virginia had fallen out of the "Reality Tree" and no emergency hospitalization was needed. In fact, they each have a solid grasp of what life is all about.

Driving home that evening I prayed that God would give me Ray's eyes – eyes to see when others need help and humor; eyes that do not miss the blessings of the simple things around me each day.

Especially, O Lord, give me Ray's vision – that rare gift of seeing beyond the old buzzards that seem to surround me. Help me, instead, to recognize that within each of us there lives a majestic eagle just waiting to soar with the strength and majesty only You can provide.

> *He gives strength to the weary*
> *and increases the power of the weak.*
> *Even youth grow tired and weary,*
> *and young men stumble and fall;*
> *But those who hope in the Lord*
> *will renew their strength.*
> *They will soar on wings like eagles;*
> *they will run and not grow weary,*
> *they will walk and not be faint.*
>
> *--Isaiah 40:29-31*

Georgianna, the Fabulous!

*W*hen I first met Georgianna Biggs she was wearing leopard skin. I strongly suspect she killed the animal herself. Though only five years old, I am sure Georgianna could hold her own against any wild beast that might cross her path.

I also suspect that while still in the womb, Georgianna was already opinionated and self-assured. Today she is a tough, indomitable kindergartener – a small package of limitless mischief looking for a place to land. Very few people intimidate her and, though she may appear shy at first, she can silence you with a glance. She quickly determines whom she trusts and distrusts. You never have to doubt where you stand with Georgianna because she speaks her mind with certainty.

Nevertheless, there is a tender touch of vulnerability and sensitivity that Georgianna displays on rare occasions – sporadic moments when you almost forget that she can be as forceful as a tornado in a trailer park.

As pretty as she is spirited, Georgianna has dark eyes that speak volumes and seem to change colors with her moods. When inevitably faced with discipline, she cuts her eyes toward you and flashes a sugary smile that, no doubt, has prevented, or at least softened, many a reprimand. And when she gently snuggles into your lap and rests her head against you, she steals your heart. In those priceless moments, it is impossible to believe that Georgianna Biggs is anything less than a beautiful blond cherub.

But there are plenty who would warn you otherwise.

Five-year-old Eric is one of those. As they played together one summer day, Georgianna suddenly became angry with Eric. No one knows why. These things just happen where Georgianna is concerned. A group of neighborhood moms, including my friend, Lauren, mother of the legendary Georgianna, chatted as their children played. The day was wonderful and without incident until Eric, crying vigorously, ran to his mom who, as luck would have it, was sitting next to Lauren.

"What's the matter, Eric? Are you hurt?" his mother inquired urgently.

Speaking so that the entire world could hear, Eric announced between tears, "Georgianna just told me to kiss her behind!"

Embarrassed beyond belief, Lauren turned a lovely shade of crimson and immediately sought out Georgianna.

Unfortunately, the story gets worse for two reasons. Number one, when told to apologize to Eric, Georgianna flatly refused. And, number two – Georgianna, in reality, did not use the word "behind." (Use your imagination, okay?)

But that is Georgianna – a beautiful little spitfire whom I can't help but love . . . perhaps because she reminds me so much of myself.

☒☒☒☒☒☒☒

Lauren and her husband, David, recently enjoyed a Saturday night on the town. Needing a babysitter, Lauren placed a call to her mother, Shirley. Known as *Mimi* to her grandchildren, this is one woman who loves spending time with her granddaughters. Though she realized Georgianna

120

would be part of the package, Mimi bravely put on her grandmother hat and agreed to sit with Georgianna and her two sisters, Lydia and Alyssa. Because Georgianna's antics are legendary both inside and outside the family, Mimi was somewhat hesitant. But she sincerely loves her grandchildren – all three – and wanted to spend time with them.

Mimi arrived around 4:00 p.m. and spent some time with her granddaughters before Lauren and David left for the evening. Georgianna sported her angelic personality and was amazingly well behaved. All proceeded smoothly and Mimi relaxed a bit. Maybe the evening would be a good one . . .

But, Lauren and David had barely left the driveway when Georgianna's other personality burst forth. She whined, grabbed toys, demanded attention, and became downright temperamental. Georgianna refused to eat dinner and pouted when Mimi placed food in front of her. Mimi recognized the direction the night was taking, but she remained calm. She played games, read books and talked with the girls, all the while standing firm in her discipline of Georgianna. But as the night wore on, Mimi's patience wore thin.

When she had enough, Mimi announced that bedtime had arrived. After warm baths and fresh pajamas, she prepared each of her three granddaughters for a peaceful night's sleep. Baby Alyssa took her bottle and was snoozing within minutes. Mimi then gathered Lydia and Georgianna so they could say their prayers before scurrying to their beds.

Everyone knows Lydia and Georgianna have completely different personalities. With a consistently sweet temperament and loving spirit, Lydia loves to snuggle and show her affection for everyone. Even at her young age, Lydia is quite sincere about her faith and, when asked to pray, does so seriously and with great fervor. That night Lydia prayed for her parents, her grandparents, a variety of aunts, uncles, friends, and minor acquaintances. She prayed for her pets, her friends at school and church, plus every person who has an influence in her young life. Lydia prayed for her swim team, her soccer team, including all coaches and participants. She thanked God for her food, her family, and her home. After an hour or two, Mimi heard Lydia's final "amen."

Turning to Georgianna, Mimi softly said, "Okay, you're next. Now you can say your prayers."

With a typical toss of her head, Georgianna advised her grandmother she did not wish to pray.

Mimi spoke softly, "You need to always say your prayers and talk to God before you go to bed."

"No," Georgianna stated emphatically.

"Well," Mimi calmly said, "why don't I say a prayer for you?"

Caring very little what happened, Georgianna allowed her grandmother to say a prayer on her behalf.

"Thank you, God, for my beautiful granddaughter, Georgianna. Thank you for her parents and her friends. Thank you for loving her. And I pray, dear Lord, that you will help Georgianna to be a good girl."

Before Mimi said "amen," the very opinionated Georgianna Biggs spoke.

"A good girl? I don't want to be good," Georgianna informed all who were listening. "I don't want to be good at all. I want to be *FABULOUS!*"

And so she is – five years old and fabulous.

Furthermore, do you realize that Georgianna Biggs speaks the truth?

God wants us each of us to have and to experience the very best life has to offer. God created a world filled with bluebirds and butterflies, tall trees and tiny flowers, sweet strawberries and tart apples. His gift of creation includes the rhythm of the tides, the sparkle of starlight, and the precision of the planets in their orbits. An entire world is ours to explore – one filled with snow-capped mountains, craggy glaciers, deep oceans and towering waterfalls. We are blessed with friends who joyously make us laugh and hold us when we weep. We have been given the very Son of God to show us the face of our Creator who, despite His greatness and majesty, still knows us by name and allows us to call him *Father.*

We worship a God who is far more than good. He's fabulous! And God wants us to turn to him, to pray, to listen, and to follow him in the paths of righteousness. Then we will experience the true blessings of the children of God – blessings of unconditional love, blessings of peace, hope, and joy to sustain us through every day, week, and year of our lives.

Georgianna, in her spirited and clever way, already knows what many of us need to learn.

Good? Think again!

God doesn't want us just to be good. God wants us to be fabulous!

I have come
that you might have life
and
have it more abundantly.

--John 10:10

I love my friend,
Marty Webb.
He is like an older brother to me.
In fact, he is so old . . .

. . . that
when Cain murdered Abel,
Marty
was called for
jury duty!.

Moments

There's
many a good tune
played on
an old fiddle.

--Samuel Butler
(1835-1902)

I sneezed rather suddenly
the other day –
a hearty sneeze that came
from the very depths
of my being.

Now I have a whole new
appreciation for
Depends
Undergarments!

Give Me a Friend On Whom I Can Depend

(Warning: For Women Only!)

*A*unt Flo first visited me a few days after my twelfth birthday. I took an instant dislike to her. But that made no difference because I knew that Aunt Flo would visit me again and again – basically every twenty-eight days for the greater part of my life. She rarely comes alone. Typically she brings other members of her family – bloating, irritability, backaches, and cramps.

This normal biological occurrence is a rite of passage shepherding a young girl into puberty and womanhood. It is necessary for the very continuation of our species. Yet for all its nobleness, I have never spoken to a woman who really enjoys this experience. In fact, Aunt Flo is one of the nicer names bestowed upon this bodily function. Other creative references include "The Curse," "The Eagle Has Landed," "The Visitor," "The Period," and "Hormonal Hell."

So, now do you know what I am talking about?

Women discuss Aunt Flo by phone, fax, and e-mail – over lunch, in gyms, at parties, and in grocery store lines. Jokes abound in sitcoms, late-night talk shows, movies, and music. Commercials advertise an infinite assortment of products

127

designed specifically to tackle this issue. Magazine ads offer coupons as incentives to purchase their merchandise. Pictures of these hygiene products are paraded on billboards and the sides of city buses. Shelves of books discuss Aunt Flo's many characteristics along with medical and emotional issues affecting women during this time. Billions of dollars are spent each year as huge companies hire thousands of individuals for research and development of new goods and merchandise. Aunt Flo has even changed our vocabulary, adding words such as minis, maxis, absorbency, Midol, and Toxic Shock Syndrome to our lexicon. Men discuss Aunt Flo and bemoan the fact that they have to deal with emotional women during "that time of the month." (Personally, I have no sympathy at all for these guys – I believe that spending just one month with Aunt Flo would have them howling for mercy.)

Without question, Aunt Flo is a royal pain. She is an author of chaos and women suffer from her antics in varying degrees. Perhaps women who suffer most are those bidding farewell to Aunt Flo. Hormonal changes take place at certain ages that directly affect Aunt Flo's monthly behavior. Some women enjoy quick visits while others endure a lengthy stopover. Quite often, Aunt Flo grows in intensity when she lingers. In fact, her force and passion may be so tremendous that she causes women to feel uncomfortable, embarrassed, and to suffer, well, leakage. These are times when women are afraid to sit, stand, or even move. Clothing, linens, and seats may be sullied as Aunt Flo releases her tremendous energy.

Recently, I endured such a visit. And, as often happens, this hormonal hell began while I was in Kentucky for a week of speaking engagements and book-signings. Aunt Flo is famous for visiting at the most inconvenient times. To say the least, I was inconvenienced. To say the most, I was aggravated and extremely self-conscious.

Mimi Smith, my practical yet progressive friend, accompanied me on this particular trip. Being the same age, we are both marching toward menopause, thus our adventures with Aunt Flo are quite similar. Like other baby-boomers, we

128

are currently enduring her unpredictability and occasional energetic eruptions. Fed up with Aunt Flo, clear-thinking Mimi decided to fight back with drastic measures.

I must pause here and speak candidly regarding certain items known as Depends Undergarments. These articles have my blessing. In fact, I believe them to be effective and indispensable to certain persons who occasionally encounter, well, leakage of another kind. It is not just the elderly who have this problem. Catastrophes can occur at any age. Having said this, I never anticipated having an interest in these items until I reached a very advanced age – most likely the age at which Willard Scott would display my photo on a Smucker's Jar during the *Today Show.*

No so for Mimi Smith. Far braver than I, Mimi grew weary of Aunt Flo's intensity. Standing before a grocery shelf one evening, Mimi reached for her typical monthly provisions. When turning to leave, though, she noticed a large colorful package just a few feet away. Two words were printed in large fuchsia letters: *Depends Undergarments.* Out of sheer curiosity, Mimi looked closer and noticed that these undergarments were designed to protect adults from, well, leakage. Though designed for a different reason altogether, Mimi wondered that, perhaps, these items just might assist her in her struggle with Aunt Flo. In complete desperation, Mimi purchased a package of said undergarments even though she is in no way ready to have her photo displayed by Willard Scott on the back of a Smucker's jar during the *Today Show.*

I ask that you not judge Mimi too harshly. Please understand that this action was made under duress because of her concern for, well, leakage related to Aunt Flo. Also, Mimi is a friend of mine who was seeking an effective solution to a problem faced by millions of women daily. Furthermore, I ask that you not judge Mimi because she shared her knowledge with me while we toured Kentucky for a week of speaking engagements and book-signings.

Put yourself in my place. During each of these events, I was center stage and knew all eyes were on me, which is stressful even under the best of circumstances. But during this week I was enormously concerned about my own, well, leakage. I was to speak to women who, undoubtedly, would understand my situation. Still, I wanted complete protection so I drove quickly to a local grocery store to purchase my monthly provisions.

Mimi, smiling slyly, accompanied me.

Walking to the appropriate aisle, I rapidly loaded my cart with a variety of products – minis and maxis in an assortment of shapes and sizes. Surely something would provide the security I needed.

Mimi, meanwhile, wandered down the aisle where I found her staring at a large colorful package. Two words were printed in large fuchsia letters: *Depends Undergarments.*

"Oh no," I thought to myself, "surely she is not thinking that I should . . ."

Mimi grabbed the package and uttered three horrifying words, "It is time."

No words can sufficiently describe my feelings at that moment. I was repulsed and disgusted. I flatly refused to consider the possibility.

"I am young, a mere babe, still practically a teenager," I whined.

Speaking quietly but passionately, I informed Mimi that I was only forty-six years old, far too young to wear a nursing home diaper. Using vivid language, I made my feelings crystal clear. In short, I sweetly advised Mimi that, while these may be exceptional products, they were certainly not for me.

"Cathy, it's time."

We stood in the adult diaper aisle arguing whether or not I should purchase a package. Simply holding the package made me age ten years. Plus, deciding what to purchase was a monumental task. The shelves held *Depends* as well as brands whose names I did not recognize. Packages were designated absorbent, super-absorbent, or ultra-absorbent. Some garments were fastened with Velcro while others were bulky pads. Still others were genuine adult-sized panties. Sizes varied greatly and I had no idea which size to purchase . . . if I ever intended on wearing such an item.

I mentioned the sizing dilemma to Mimi, assuming that would end the discussion. The size I would wear depended on my waist measurement and, in the middle of a Kentucky Kroger at 10:00 p.m., I had no way of determining such a measurement. Or so I thought.

Mimi spoke again.

"Not so fast."

In shock and amazement I watched Mimi Smith reach into her purse and, with a fiendish sneer, pull out a tape measure. A tape measure! I knew that Mimi was famous for always having a sewing or home improvement project on the drawing board, but I never knew that a tape measure lived in her purse. I could not believe my eyes. Even worse, I could not believe my ears when I realized the thing was retractable and, therefore, clicked loudly as she pulled the tape from its plastic canister. The sound echoed throughout the Kentucky Kroger, from frozen foods to the bakery. Before I knew what was happening, that witch Mimi was wrapping the tape around my waist to secure a measurement – right in the middle of an out-of-state grocery store. I could only imagine that all security cameras immediately turned in our direction.

My only stroke of luck was that we were in unfamiliar territory. What were the odds that anyone would know me? And what were the odds that anyone who knew me would walk down the Depends aisle of a Kentucky Kroger at 10:00 p.m. while Mimi held a tape measure around my waist.

Do not, I repeat, do not underestimate my capacity to be humiliated.

Glen Rogers rounded the corner at this moment. I had no idea that a friend from my days in Graduate School lived in this small town. And as luck would have it, he just happened to be doing some late-night shopping this very same Kentucky Kroger!

I ask again, "What are the odds?"

"Cathy!" he practically shouted. "Is that you?"

Oh yes, it was me – motionless, red-faced, standing in front of the adult diapers with a friend holding a retractable tape measure strapped around my waist. Mimi froze, which I suppose explains why she continued to clutch the tape measure instead of quickly returning it to her purse. Sick with embarrassment, I fully expected Glen to ask questions or at least glance uncomfortably at my cart filled with monthly provisions and adult undergarments.

But the topic was never broached. Glen only discussed the church he was serving, his recent divorce, a new car, and his surprise at finding me at 10:00 p.m. in his neighborhood Kentucky Kroger store. Watching him closely, I realized that he was not simply being nice to avoid an awkward moment. Glen was absorbed in his own life and did not take note of the obvious circumstances – where we were standing or that a tape measure encircled my waist. He continued to talk and even invited me to speak to his church congregation. Smiling, I returned the small talk but was relieved to bid him farewell.

Glen left and for perhaps the first time in my life, I thanked God for a self-absorbed, clueless man.

"Quick," Mimi whispered. "Grab the Depends."

"What size?" I asked.

"Get the large – you don't need the extra large."

Well, at least that was a blessing.

⧗⧗⧗⧗⧗⧗⧗

Without going into great detail, let me say that upon returning to the hotel, I heeded the advice of my friend, Mimi Smith, the practical-minded tape measure fanatic. That evening, to my surprise and amazement, I slept peacefully for the first time in three nights. Why? Because I no longer had to worry about, well, leakage.

I made my peace with Depends Undergarments because I am not using them for their intended purpose. I do not have that particular aging problem yet. Still I have Aunt Flo who continues to visit me monthly to disrupt my hormones and my life.

Well, Aunt Flo, you may still be a presence in my life, but your days are numbered. And though you remain, you will no longer destroy my poise and confidence. I am no longer overly concerned with your strength and power and I will, yea verily, sleep peacefully at night.

Furthermore, I will proudly share my experience and knowledge with other frustrated women. In fact, please allow me to testify regarding two things I realized late one night in a Kentucky Kroger.

Ladies, as God is my witness, Mimi Smith has revolutionized my life.

And, once again, a man remained clueless.

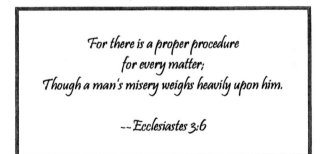

For there is a proper procedure
for every matter;
Though a man's misery weighs heavily upon him.

-- Ecclesiastes 3:6

Serious Porch Sitting

Supper dishes done and the kitchen floor swept, she wearily walked toward the front porch. The screen door made its usual screech then a loud slam as the rusty spring closed it quickly behind her. She lowered herself onto the white iron swing and a weary sigh escaped her lips. She acknowledged her fatigue and marveled at how being "just a housewife and mother" could consume her day. How good it was to finally have a few moments alone.

"Hey Emma, Mama's on the porch."

So much for her time alone.

Her daughters raced to join her, scrambling to see who would sit beside her. Instinctively she moved toward the center of the swing, making room for them to sit on either side. As they snuggled next to her, the youngest toddled onto the porch, barefoot, her bellybutton peeking over the top of a diaper, holding a bottle of apple juice in one hand. The toddler climbed onto the swing and found a comfortable niche in her mother's lap.

Placing both of her tired feet on the cool concrete floor, the mother pushed the swing in a slow rhythmic motion. She began to hum softly, so softly that all three daughters had to hush themselves to hear the music. Mama mostly hummed songs from the brown Cokesbury hymnal at church, but there were others as well. Occasionally she would sing softly about Aunt Rhodie and the Old Grey Goose. Mama continued the music, confident that the sound and the motion of the old swing would quiet them until they fell asleep.

But the rusty creak of the porch swing and clamor of the crickets kept them awake.

"Look at the lightening bugs, Mama," Emma jumped up quickly, disturbing the peaceful setting. "Can I get a jar and catch some?"

"Not right now," Mama replied. "Let's just sit and enjoy watching them."

Ella, three years younger, spoke up, "I'd sure like to know how those lightening bugs work. I'll bet if you catch a whole jar full, you could use it as a flashlight."

"That's stupid," Emma replied, beginning yet another argument between the sisters.

Daddy joined them on the porch, seating himself in an old yellow chair that squeaked in harmony with the old porch swing. Mama hummed louder and the sisters grew quiet. From the porch swing they all studied the brilliant sunset – the colors, the shapes, the designs. They pondered mysterious questions such as, "Where did God get His crayons?" and, "What are His favorite colors?"

They played cloud games, looking for their favorite animals and shapes in the evening sky. By the time the 9:45 train whistled in the distance, the toddler was sleeping and the older girls were struggling to keep their eyes open.

Mama and Daddy talked quietly about everyday things. Ella needed a new pair of shoes. Emma was going to a birthday party Saturday afternoon. The okra needed to be picked tomorrow and a few green tomatoes were perfect for frying. The newborn calf was doing well. Homecoming was Sunday at the Methodist Church and Mama would take some fried chicken and pineapple sandwiches.

All the girls were asleep by now. Mama carried the toddler while Daddy steered Emma and Ella toward their beds.

After locking the doors and taking a quick, cool bath, Mama sat down on the edge of the bed. Turning the lamp off, she lay down, pulled the clean, sun-dried sheet over her tired body and listened to the sounds of the night. The man next to her snored gently while the children slept soundly in their beds.

She closed her eyes in weariness and whispered a quiet prayer of thanksgiving to the God who blessed them with health, happiness, and a home. Mama listened briefly to the lullaby of the crickets before drifting into a comforting sleep.

They all slept soundly that night, comfortable and content, secure in the happy blessing of being a family.

The Lord bless you and keep you;
the Lord make his face shine upon you
and be gracious to you;
the Lord turn his face toward you
and give you peace.

--Numbers 6:24-26

*Is
God
married
to
Mother Nature?*

--Carlee, Age 8

Living in Love's Shadow

*A*mbushed and knocked for a-winding!   That is what happened to me last Christmas Eve.

To be honest, I had a touch of the Holiday Blues. Those of us who have lost loved ones are acutely aware of their absence, especially amid the sweet season of Christmas. My prescription? Stay busy. I attended church activities, partied with friends and colleagues, and accomplished my shopping, wrapping, and baking. (Yes, baking. I do have my domestic moments, but I try to keep them to a minimum).

Though I was sufficiently distracted, my holiday schedule was not appreciated by the one who now shares my home – a cheerful, golden-haired canine named Shadow. I do not know if dogs suffer from the Holiday Blues, but I can assure you that Shadow certainly did not like my frantic pace. Not at all! He was not receiving a sufficient amount of attention and he was not happy. He wanted my full attention . . . immediately.

Shadow's former address was the Cherokee County Humane Society. I adopted him almost two years ago when he was just the cute little dog in pen number three. After his adoption I quickly scheduled his first visit to the vet. I still remember the doctor's words, "Shadow is healthy and seems to be just over one year old. He probably will not grow much larger than he is now."

Not!

Faithfully consuming his Wal-Mart Old Roy dog food, Shadow quickly left behind his medium-sized body and matured into a creature resembling a small horse.

So it was Christmas Eve when this creature – part dog, part horse, part human – expressed his displeasure with the busy schedule that kept me from playing with him.

I stepped onto the patio that evening and walked in the direction of the Wal-Mart Old Roy dog food. In the spirit of good fun, Shadow swiftly ran toward me. With the momentum he had gained, the dog was unable to stop his 90-pound body. He knocked me to the ground and immediately pounced upon me for some Christmas Eve horseplay.

(Note to Self: Consider buying low-fat dog food).

He held no ill will toward me, of course. He simply had been alone too long and wanted to have some fun.

(Note to Self: Consider adopting a second dog to keep Shadow from being so lonely).

Lying on the cold ground, I covered my face to protect myself from his razor-sharp toenails.

(Note to Self: Does Spa Sydell offer doggie pedicures?).

The creature bombarded me with slimy kisses while doggie drool dripped onto my face and into my hair.

(Note to Self: Locate a store that sells Doggie Bibs).

I struggled to stand, but found that to be impossible with a 90-pound dog/horse sitting on my stomach. So I remained pinned to the December ground with a sharp boulder wedged between my fourth and fifth vertebrae.

(Note to Self: OUCH!).

Meanwhile, dog drool garnished my hair.

(Note to Self: Use high-octane shampoo tonight).

From my unique view I suddenly glanced at Shadow and saw a look of complete exultation on his face. He loved me! And he craved love in return. Love, perhaps the most powerful force in the universe, was at my disposal in the form of a 90-pound happy, golden dog.

(Note to Self: I would rather this be Dylan McDermott, but I cannot expect a Christmas miracle of that magnitude).

Wrestling free, I lifted my arms and gave Shadow a big hug as I began to laugh . . . out loud.

(Note to Self: Never mind what the neighbors think).

Despite the cold temperatures and my long to-do list, I took the time to play. I threw a green ball with a bell inside it across the yard and laughed as Shadow jumped, caught it, and swung his head from left to right to make the bell jingle. He chewed the ball until the bell disappeared into the frozen grass.

(Note to Self: Buy a new green ball with a bell inside).

I chased him around in circles until I fell over from dizziness.

(Note to Self: Don't do THAT again).

Finally, exhausted, I sat with his head in my lap until the sun slept and the stars lit the heavens that Christmas Eve night. What an unexpected gift I had received. For a few precious moments I was a child, a ten-year-old playing and laughing with no concern other than the sweet anticipation of a magical Christmas Eve. My Holiday Blues eased and, in a gesture of thanks, I turned my face toward the heavens.

Ambushed and knocked for a-winding! That is what happened to me on New Year's Eve.

I fell victim to a wicked stomach virus. Instead of laughing and playing, I spent the day in front of the fireplace in an old flannel gown with a bottle of Pepto Bismol in one hand and a plastic garbage can clutched to my chest. I was no longer a laughing ten-year-old. No! I was a pale, aching, dizzy old woman with a severe case of fever, chills, and a heaving stomach.

And so the cycle goes. Joy and sorrow . . . frustration and happiness . . . good and bad . . . ecstasy and grief . . . old and new. Our days are filled with all of these things, you know. That is the way of life. But it is the way of God to be with us during each of the moments.

Praise Him for His precious daily presence.

Now, go play.

*To him who is able to keep you from falling
and to present you before his glorious presence
without fault and with great joy –
to the only God our Savior
be glory, majesty, power and authority,
through Jesus Christ our Lord,
before all ages, now and forevermore.
Amen.*

--Jude 1:24

Staring at the Black

*C*heck your dictionary. Her photograph might be found next to any number of words – precocious, gifted, feisty, or funny. The classic strong-willed child, Kerry radiates confidence and independence. She is a five-year-old bundle of attitude and assurance. A beautiful little girl, Kerry's petite body is crowned with flowing blonde hair that evokes an image of a princess dressed in pink surrounded by dolls and tea sets.

But Kerry will quickly inform you that she doesn't "do" pink. She is far more comfortable in red cowboy boots, a leather jacket, or a soccer uniform.

The daughter of my friends, Dick and Jennifer Huycke, Kerry has always had a strong personality. Even at her young age she holds strong opinions on most any subject . . . and most any person. I can proudly say that Kerry and I are friends and, believe me, that was no easy accomplishment for me. Suspicious at first, Kerry follows her instincts and learns to trust before inviting you into her heart.

Now that she is my buddy, Kerry loves to wake me when I spend the night with the Huycke family. Unlike me, she is a dynamo by daybreak and simply cannot understand my long-held conviction that God created Saturday mornings for sleeping late.

Recently, I spent the night at Kerry's house. Saturday dawned – a gray, rainy, and cold day. It was a morning when all God's children should have been snuggling beneath a warm

143

blanket and a couple of quilts. The house was quiet and I was sleeping nicely until I heard the creak of the bedroom door. Opening one eye, I spied Kerry peering at me. Seeing my one open eye, Kerry realized I was somewhat conscious. She entered the room and watched me. Struggling to open both eyes, I watched her back.

Suddenly, she placed her hands on her tiny hips, cocked her head and declared, "Cathy, you are staring at me!"

"I'm not staring. I was just looking to see who was coming into the room," I countered defensively. (This kid scares me.)

"Well, you are looking at me now. And you've looked at me long enough for it to be a stare."

Help me, Lord!

"I promise not to stare at you anymore," and I closed my eyes, assuming she would go find her cowboy boots or leather jacket or a Harley to ride (or possibly a Sunday School teacher to beat up!)

Before falling asleep, though, I heard her voice again.

"Cathy, your eyes are closed. Now you are staring at the black."

That did it! I laughed out loud. By golly, I was indeed staring at the black. How could I argue with her? And who would want to argue with her? Hearing my laughter, she jumped onto the bed and I was soon playing and laughing with smart and sassy Kerry Huycke.

Staring at the black. Has anyone caught you doing that recently?

I have done it many times. It is easy to forget our blessings when troubles seem overwhelming. My husband died several years ago and I became a widow at the age of thirty-five. For a long time I stared at nothing but the black. Like most, I have experienced family tensions, financial struggles, health scares, and broken relationships. The world is a frightening place these days with wars and rumors of wars. Often I am lonely and afraid, traveling a road with bumps, curves, and far too many unexpected twists and turns.

Believe me, I can stare at the black with the best of 'em.

We may be Christians, but that does not shield us from the tough times of life. There are those of us called into ministry, but that does not keep us from having our black moments. Though I am now a professional speaker, writer, singer, and event leader, at times I still catch myself staring at the black.

But with age and experience comes the wisdom to know that even the black can be redemptive. I diligently seek to accept my moments of black and learn from them. I happily share my struggles because they may be your struggles as well. And perhaps we can learn from one another to open our eyes a little wider, look past the black, and focus on the Light of the World – the ever-present and eternal Light who is always with us even when it seems the Light has been extinguished forever.

The black moments will come but the Light has always been, and will always be, stronger than the darkness of fear, depression, loneliness, and anxiety.

You might not know my friend Kerry Huycke, the precocious and feisty strong-willed child with the red cowboy boots and the sassy attitude who also happens to be a pretty good five-year-old philosopher and theologian. You can still heed her words, however.

Are you staring at the black? Well, open your eyes a little wider and look around. You might just find the face of love staring back.

> *The people who walked in darkness have seen a great light.*
>
> *-- Isaiah 9:2*

Oh!

So that is what
Metamucil
is
for!

Barbeque, Brunswick Stew and Fried Apple Pies

"**S**o, Cathy, you are from Newnan, Georgia?"
Now that I am traveling a great deal, this is a question I am often asked.

"Yes," I answer. Then I wait, knowing that three inevitable questions are bound to follow:

- *Do you know Alan Jackson or Doug Stone?*
- *Did you ever meet Lewis Grizzard?*
- *Have you eaten at Sprayberry's Barbeque?*

Well, of course I have eaten at Sprayberry's Barbeque. You cannot call yourself a true Newnanite until you have feasted on barbeque pork and Brunswick Stew at this world-famous establishment. I think this mandate exists somewhere in the by-laws of both Newnan and Coweta County, Georgia.

Sadly, though, I never had the good fortune to meet dear ole Lewis. However, I once stumbled upon a story that included three of his favorite topics – Newnan, Sprayberry's and Yankees. Lewis, no doubt, would have written a wonderfully humorous and touching account of this event. I would have enjoyed reading that story. But, alas, Lewis is no longer with us – a unique talent and voice of the south who left us far too soon.

Therefore, in his memory, allow me to relay a scandalous incident that took place in my very own hometown of Newnan, Georgia.

Not long ago I vacationed in Destin, Florida, with my friend, Toni Jernigan. I met Toni in 1980 when, as a member of the Staff Parish Relations Committee of Grace United Methodist Church, she was part of a group that interviewed me for a position on the staff of this celebrated church. The good news? I got the job. The even better news? Toni (plus her husband, Bill, and sons, Wade and Keith) became lifelong friends.

Our friendship wavered, though, when Toni and I drove home from Destin, Florida, on that hot summer afternoon. As we neared Newnan, our growling stomachs signaled that dinnertime was approaching. We noticed a billboard advertising world-famous Sprayberry's Barbeque and realized the restaurant was only minutes away. Just then Toni spoke up, uttering an unbelievable statement – one that still haunts me to this day.

"I've never eaten at Sprayberry's Barbeque."

What? I almost ran off the road. My heart pounded and I felt I would be overcome with the vapors! (Vapors – a southern term meaning to feel faint or woozy. It most certainly is a cause for using smelling salts). And I called this woman my friend? Toni and her family have traveled the world yet she had never eaten at Sprayberry's in Newnan? I was speechless and dazed by this revelation. I never realized Toni Jernigan, my good friend, was so culturally challenged. I had to take charge.

Acting quickly, I shifted into warp speed, took the Newnan exit on two wheels and screeched to a stop in the Sprayberry's parking lot. Opening the screen door, we walked inside and settled at a table near the window.

Toni's eyes widened as she explored the mouth-watering menu – barbeque pork, beef, ribs, and luscious desserts. Though she struggled with her decision, she finally ordered the ever-popular pork plate.

As we relaxed and anticipated our forthcoming culinary pleasure, two gentlemen entered the restaurant and took a table next to ours. Their obvious dialect told me straight away that they weren't from these parts.

Yankees! In Sprayberry's Barbeque!

Immediately I recalled Aunt Pittypat from Margaret Mitchell's great southern classic *Gone With The Wind*. A nervous woman at best, Aunt Pittypat suffered from anxiety, fear, and a terminal case of the vapors. Thus, she never went anywhere without her smelling salts. You can only imagine her panic as the Civil War brought the northern army closer to her serene southern home. As Sherman's army entered Atlanta amid booming cannons and leaping flames, Aunt Pittypat was shaking and crying at what seemed to be the end of her world. In a complete tizzy, a panicky Aunt Pittypat uttered what is perhaps my favorite movie line of all times:

"Yankees in Georgia? How did they ever get in?"

I shared Aunt Pittypat's sentiments as we overheard one of the men whisper, "What is Brunswick Stew?"

Toni and I gasped and felt as though we needed smelling salts of our own.

"Let's not judge them too harshly," I said. "Brunswick Stew is a southern dish. After all, I don't eat clam chowder or oyster dressing."

Regaining her composure, Toni (the Sprayberry's rookie) spoke to these Yankee gentlemen, kindly explaining the savory blend of the slow-cooked meats, vegetables and tomato base that is Brunswick Stew. Though very tempted, I decided not to share the fact that the tender meat of a boiled hog's head quite often is a chief ingredient of this southern delight. While true, I believe this fact would have shocked and traumatized these men so completely that, no doubt, there would have been two dead Yankee carcasses littering the Sprayberry's dining room floor. In the interest of North/South relations, I forced myself to keep my mouth shut. (Sometimes I regret that!)

Turning to our own dinner, Toni and I feasted on tender pork barbeque with all the fixings. We felt terrific and even considered forgiving these northern gentlemen for their lack of knowledge regarding life in the south. Our forgiveness, though, seemed a bit premature when, eyeing the dessert menu, the same man whispered, "What is a fried apple pie?"

I motioned for the smelling salts. Okay, I gave them the benefit of the doubt regarding the Brunswick Stew. But this question was just too much and I blurted, "WHAT IS A FRIED APPLE PIE? IT'S FRIED! IT'S APPLE! IT'S A PIE! WHAT PART OF THAT DON'T YOU UNDERSTAND?"

After a moment of stunned silence, I want you to know that those Yankees began laughing.

"That was a rather silly question," Yankee number one admitted. "Fried apple pie is pretty clear and straightforward. It tells me all I need to know."

And this kind man treated all of us to fried apple pies – plus ice cream!

While I am reasonably sure that Jesus never dined at Sprayberry's, I believe he would have thought the food quite "heavenly."

Jesus Christ was the Son of God. But He was also a man who saw beauty in the simplicity of life: The lilies of the field. The birds of the air. The laughter of a child. I think Jesus would have genuinely enjoyed a Sprayberry's fried apple pie.

Fried. Apple. Pie. Three words so deliciously simple.

And Jesus would have enjoyed the friendship that was forged that night between two gentlemen from the north and two daughters of the south.

After all, it was Jesus who spoke three other simple little words – words so clear and straightforward they are meant to guide our actions and our very lives:

"Love One Another."

Now, what part of that don't we understand?

> *Above all,
> love each other deeply,
> because love
> covers a multitude of sins.*
>
> *--1 Peter 4:8*

Daybreak

Out of the shadows of night
The world rolls into light;
It is daybreak everywhere.

--Henry Wadsworth Longfellow
(1807-1882)
Written March 15, 1882 --
Nine days before his death.

*Dear Lord,
If I have done
any good in my life,
let this be my reward . . .*

*Please,
do not let me die
on the toilet!*

The Beauty of Death

Dedicated with love to Michele Salle

*T*he drive to Lake Junaluska, North Carolina, was awash with the beauty of autumn. While the foliage was stunning in Atlanta, it became even more majestic as I approached the mountains. The leaves reflected all the colors of the season – fiery reds, deep maroons, bright golds, brilliant oranges. The hues blended to make the trip a spiritual experience and I found myself thanking God for the incredible beauty of autumn, my favorite season of the year.

For the fourth weekend in a row I was traveling to Lake Junaluska near Maggie Valley, North Carolina. The Southeastern Jurisdictional Headquarters of the United Methodist Church, Lake Junaluska Assembly is a picture-perfect setting for a spiritual retreat. Tall mountains surround a shimmering lake and beautifully landscaped grounds. I am at Lake Junaluska frequently each spring and fall to lead retreats for various churches in the southeast. This particular year, I was booked for retreats every weekend in October. These weekly drives allowed me to observe the progression of autumn. The color grew more dazzling each day and, by the fourth weekend, the scenery was glorious.

Autumn has always been my favorite time of year. A unique crispness fills the air. A simple mound of leaves becomes a natural playground for children and adults. Darkness falls early and fireplaces come alive, filling homes with a cozy, comfortable glow. This is a time for sweaters, boots, football games, and homecoming dances. It is a traditional prelude to the holiday season.

The most prominent characteristic of autumn has to be the leaves. They appear in all shapes and sizes as their brilliant tones adorn city streets and country roads. They are perhaps most beautiful when covering mountainsides with their glittering shades. Many people make annual pilgrimages to the mountains, seeking front row seats for one of nature's most beloved performances.

My late October drive to Lake Junaluska was crammed with such sights. Every curve, every bend in the road featured a scene more astonishing than the one before. But as I celebrated the majesty of nature, I was suddenly struck, practically paralyzed, with a staggering truth – *I was looking into the face of death.*

The leaves were dying.

The magnificent colors of fall existed only because, in dying, leaves from a multitude of trees were being transformed from life-affirming green to deep autumn hues. This realization was overwhelming and I felt uneasy and somewhat betrayed. I was reluctant to admit that death was such a prominent part of my favorite time of year. In fact, the season is beautiful, in large part, because of the reality of death. Yet I could not deny the fact that leaves from the mighty oaks and maples were, even then, dying. And in dying, they produce the sights we find so breathtaking.

Autumn leaves do not choose to be beautiful. In fact, they have no control over what happens to them. They are simply playing their part in the cycle of life – surrendering their lives to make way for new growth that comes with the spring. Leaves die. But their legacy is the splendor of the season.

Death was all around me and I marveled at the beauty. At the same time, I was angry.

156

Quite frankly, I never expected to use the words *death* and *beauty* in the same sentence. After all, I have lost many people to death and, in moments of intense grief, it is unthinkable that beauty can be found in death. On the contrary, death is frightening even for a Christian. It is physically, emotionally, and spiritually painful. It is mysterious. It is the ultimate nightmare of a control freak. We are powerless to manage what happens to us. And no one knows exactly what to expect during the actual experience of death and dying.

No one celebrates when told they have a terminal illness. It is our very nature to fight to stay alive. It is also our nature to fight to keep those we love from dying. And when death ultimately comes, grief overrides our emotions and it sounds ridiculous to assume that beauty exists anywhere in the process of dying.

But it can.

There are certain deaths I will never comprehend. I am not meant to understand. I am called to walk in faith knowing Christ is preparing a place for all who love him (John 14:1-3).

Nevertheless, I question the loss of children, so pure and innocent. I wonder why terrorists fly planes into tall towers and kill good people. I weep over the slaughter of young soldiers on battlefields. I ache for those who suffer disease and tremendous pain. I hurt for those who die quickly and violently, leaving family and friends shocked, lonely, and unable to grasp the magnitude and finality of their loss.

Death and *beauty?* No. I have suffered loss and find nothing beautiful about grieving for a person I have loved with all my heart.

My mind raced as I drove among the mountains of North Carolina. Wherever I looked, the green had fled and the leaves were red, bronze, and gold. Death encircled me.

⧗⧗⧗⧗⧗⧗⧗

Michele Salle is one of *Wednesday's Girls* – a group of terrific women I met when teaching a Disciple Class for Johns Creek United Methodist Church in Duluth, Georgia. This nine-month class gave us ample opportunity to learn all about one another as we studied and learned, laughed and cried, and consumed more muffins than any of us care to recall. Like all the women in this group, Michele is very serious about her spiritual life and her relationship with Jesus Christ.

"When I am down, reading my Bible lifts me like nothing else. It is so comforting," she recently told me.

Michele is a bright, blond bundle of energy and faith who is totally devoted to her family and church.

By the way, she is also thin and attractive but I try not to hold that against her!

She smiles her brightest when speaking of her husband, Brice, and their children, six-year-old Sydney and three-year-old Stephen.

Like the other Wednesday's Girls, Michele at first was merely a name on an e-mail list I received from the church. But when she hosted our first class in her home, I began to learn more about the person behind the name. And during the nine months we studied together, I learned a great deal about Michele as well as the other Wednesday's Girls. After a nine-month class, we evolved into a family – one that experienced all the highs and lows of life. We celebrated the healthy birth of Amy's son, Matthew, and cried when Michele's fifty-eight-year-old mom, Camille Petkevich, was diagnosed with cancer.

"I am just not ready to lose my mother yet," Michele expressed as we talked just after the diagnosis was confirmed. "We have just reached the age where my children are no longer infants and we can spend time alone when she visits. We are growing in our relationship and talk more like women and friends instead of simply mother and daughter."

Though her mother lived in Florida, Michele talked and visited with her often. That is why Camille's illness hit Michele so hard. Diagnosed with colon cancer in 2002, doctors expected Camille to make a complete recovery. However, the cancer spread. Doctors feel it probably metastasized when the original mass was surgically removed. Camille responded well at first but blood tests eventually indicated the presence of cancer somewhere in her body. But where? More tests were scheduled and, when completed, indicated the cancer was extensive. Except for her brain, cancer ran rampant throughout Camille's body.

Michele was understandably devastated and flew to Florida as her mother spoke with doctors regarding additional treatment and her uncertain future. The cancer was too advanced to stop. However, they hoped to prolong her life, perhaps as long as eighteen months, with chemotherapy. With no time to waste, the treatments began. Though early treatments went well, Camille grew weaker with each additional chemo treatment.

A mere five weeks following discovery of the advanced cancer, Camille Petkevich died at the age of fifty-eight.

As a group, Wednesday's Girls grieved with Michele and her family. We prayed, but still felt helpless because we wanted to do more for our precious friend. Her suffering became ours as well.

I could see no beauty in Camille's death. After all, fifty-eight is still young and this woman had so much to give her family, church, and community.

But as our group listened to Michele's story over our low-fat muffins one Wednesday morning, we began to see a different perspective – one that reminded us that God was constantly with Camille and her faith held strong.

Michele and her family had made plans to visit Camille during their spring break. They had arranged their schedules to spend ten days with Camille, her husband, and Michele's sister. Michele's brother would be coming at a later date because no one realized death would come so quickly.

Michele awoke on a Tuesday morning, several days before they were to leave for Florida. She had hardly slept because she felt a strong urging, a sense that she should go to her mother immediately, instead of waiting for spring break to

159

arrive. At first Michele attributed her feelings to worry and paranoia. As the sense of urgency continued, Brice made arrangements for Michele to fly to Florida and be at her mother's side.

God speaks to us through our thoughts and gentle nudges, as Michele soon learned. Without realizing it, Camille's death was fast approaching. By arriving early, Michele was given an incredible gift – precious, unforgettable moments with her mother. Michele slept by her mother's side for three nights before Camille was taken by ambulance to a hospice in Hollywood, Florida. For the next two days (Friday and Saturday), Camille drifted in and out of consciousness.

One of the most difficult moments for Michele came Friday night as Camille, barely conscious, fought death. She was loud and emotional as she struggled to live.

On Saturday morning, a very wise nurse entered the room. Speaking softly to Michele, the nurse shared wisdom she had gleaned from other patients.

"Your mother is holding on because of the tremendous love she feels here. Tell her to stop fighting. Let her go in love."

Through tears, Michele whispered precious words of life to her mother. "We love you, mom, but it is okay to stop fighting. Go to Jesus and he will take you home."

Summoning all her remaining energy, Camille spoke three final words: "I see Jesus."

And she was at peace.

⧗⧗⧗⧗⧗⧗

Though unconscious, Camille was the leading character in a family reunion that memorable Saturday night. In her final hours, her children surrounded her with their presence and their love. Michele, her sister, and her brother, spoke to Camille as though she were fully awake. In gentle whispers, they praised her for being a loving and devoted parent. Between tears and smiles, they recalled stories from years long gone, moments from their innocent days of childhood. Holding her hand, they spoke words of love and gratitude.

Finally, they gave Camille perhaps their greatest gift – words of release, their unselfish blessing for Camille to leave her broken body and walked into life everlasting where a new, spiritual body awaited.

As a statement of their faith, Camille's family asked their pastor to lead the family in worship at 1:00 on Sunday afternoon. The room filled with family that day and, just before 1:00, Michele gently sang *Jesus Loves Me* to her mother – just as Camille had sung to Michele so many times before. Once the familiar words faded, the family began singing that beautiful hymn that has comforted millions: *Amazing Grace! How Sweet the Sound . . . .*

Camille's family raised their voices and, in doing so, declared that, for a Christian, hope is stronger than death. Their song echoed throughout the halls of the hospice where loss is so prevalent.

At that moment, Camille's family was a community of faith sharing their conviction that "death has been swallowed up in victory" (I Corinthians 15:54b). Their song went to the very heart of many patients and staff of the hospice. Countless individuals stopped what they were doing to listen to these sweet words of faith and life.

And their song went to the very heart of Camille who, in the midst of their singing, opened her eyes and took one final, lingering look at her children and family. In the presence of love, Camille closed her eyes, shed her diseased body, and stepped into life everlasting.

"I felt incredible joy and grief at the same time," Michele shared with me. "No words are adequate to describe how I felt as I realized that thirty of us were there to gently push my mother forward into her next life. It was one of the most beautiful moments of my life!"

Beautiful?

My mind recalled the autumn leaves that are most beautiful when dying. I recalled my feelings of anger and betrayal when I realized that death was a major part of my favorite time of the year. I recalled how, with every brilliant leaf and every dazzling color, I looked into the face of death.

No, I never expected to use death and beauty in the same sentence because of the many losses I have experienced and the inevitable grief that follows. And, though unexplainable tragedy is part of life in this imperfect world, I finally realize that beauty and death can walk hand-in-hand.

When a life has been lived well and a Christian faces the end of earthly existence, it is fitting to celebrate the journey into eternity. When there is no cause to wonder about the destiny of a loved one, it is proper to rejoice. When a painful, broken body is transformed into a perfect, spiritual body, there is cause for joy. And when we realize that one day we will be reunited with those we love – never to be separated again – it is downright ridiculous not to whoop, holler, and appreciate the beauty that can be found in death.

Still, never forget that grief is natural. Yes, we are people of an empty tomb and an empty cross, but we also have empty hearts when someone we love is no longer with us. Though there is beauty, there is also pain. We hurt deeply because we have loved deeply. There are those who will tell you that a Christian should neither grieve nor weep at the death of someone we have loved immensely.

Bull!

The shortest verse in the Bible is *Jesus wept* (John 11:35). Jesus wept at the tomb of Lazarus, a friend whom he deeply loved. Even though Jesus had the power to raise Lazarus – and he did – Jesus wept because of the pain of loss. Grief is a normal response to loss. Do not confuse it with the strength of your faith.

And autumn this year? It is only weeks away and I still look forward to the brilliant colors, the cool air, sweaters and cozy fireplaces. But I will appreciate the season far more than

162

in past years. I will watch the leaves more carefully and better understand their message.

God's beauty is all around us, even in the presence of death.

The autumn leaves – and Camille – have convinced me.

*Precious in the sight of the Lord
is the death of his saints.*

-- Psalm 116:13

*Death is not
extinguishing the light --*

*It is putting
out the lamp
because the dawn has come.*

--Unknown

Swimming in the Infinity Pool

$\mathcal{D}$eborah called late one Tuesday night last summer. Because of job deadlines and a full calendar, she had taken no vacation. Summer was ending and she wanted to have some fun, even if for just one day. I felt the same way, so we concluded that a twenty-four-hour mental health break was necessary.

"If I pay, will you go to the Ritz Carlton with me?"

That is perhaps the dumbest question Deborah has ever asked.

The Ritz Carlton? Free? Even though it was only for one night, I was not about to turn down a trip to paradise. Time was too short for a drive to the Ritz Carlton at Amelia Island, Florida, (my favorite spot when I have the money – and even when I don't have the money) so we opted to visit the brand new Ritz Carlton Reynolds Plantation on Lake Oconee in Greensboro, Georgia. Just an hour's drive from Atlanta (or a three day drive if Deborah is behind the wheel), this location fit our time frame perfectly. I called and made arrangements for an early check-in and a late checkout so that our mental health break could last as long as possible.

Arriving at the hotel by noon, we were greeted by a concierge holding a silver tray with a fresh rose, glass of champagne, and a cool herbal cloth for each of us. You gotta love this place! As Deborah and I chatted and attempted to look very suave and sophisticated, the concierge pointed out the various amenities of this new resort. The hotel was home to superb restaurants, cozy sitting areas decorated with beautiful furnishings, gift shops offering everything from chocolates to Ritz Carlton souvenirs. A magnificent spa boasted an indoor pool plus several hot tubs. From reflexology massages to herbal body wraps to energizing enzyme facials, the spa provided a variety of sensual pleasures ideal for a twenty-four-hour mental health break.

While our minds were contemplating these heavenly delights, the concierge seemed most excited about a unique feature of the Ritz Carlton Reynolds Plantation.

"You must visit the infinity pool!" she raved. "It is amazing. In fact, you probably will never want to leave it." She pointed us in the direction of the famed infinity pool situated along the shores of Lake Oconee.

Deborah and I smiled, acting as if we knew just what an infinity pool was. Of course, we had no clue. But under the heat of the Georgia summer sun, any pool is a good pool, even one we knew nothing about. To settle our curiosity, we threw on our swimsuits and quickly headed toward the infinity pool, right where most of the guests seemed to be congregated.

Located on the edge of Lake Oconee, the infinity pool was indeed the happening place that sizzling summer day. It was enormous and filled with dazzling water reflecting the deep blue colors of the pool's sides and bottom. Droplets sparkled like diamonds as children and adults splashed and dipped in this wet wonderland. A host of other guests lounged and happily baked in the July sun. The setting was enchanting and the infinity pool was party central for a happy crowd of hotel guests.

At first glance, the infinity pool seemed like any other. As we moved closer, though, we noticed one significant difference. Three traditional walls restrained countless gallons of water. But the fourth side was anything but traditional. Directly facing Lake Oconee, this fourth wall featured a vanishing side. The wall was imperceptible because water constantly flowed over its blue tile and plummeted into an

166

exterior trough along the foundation of the pool. Very smart engineers and designers developed a means by which water from the trough was then cycled back into the pool.

Quite unconventional, the design gave the impression that the pool was not fully enclosed and, in fact, flowed into Lake Oconee. When standing in the middle of the pool, it seemed that the waters merged, hence giving the impression that the pool and the lake were one all-encompassing entity. In essence, it was impossible to determine where the pool ended and the lake began. It seemed as though we were swimming in both bodies of water at the same time because they became as one. I was captivated by the illusion that the infinity pool and lake were not separate, but unified – each a part of the other.

In an instant, the familiar words of the Lord's Prayer came to my mind: " . . . your kingdom come, your will be done on earth as it is in heaven" (Matthew 6:10).

How often do we repeat this phrase without fully comprehending its meaning? As Christians, our greatest desire should be to show others the face of Christ and, therefore, a glimpse of all things heavenly. There have been moments when it seemed I beheld a glimpse of heaven, perhaps through the touch of a friend, the words of a hymn, or the sound of a gentle summer rain. These moments remind me of what the world was meant to be. *On earth as it is in heaven* will only be realized when we allow the very essence of Christ to take root within our souls and blossom into the guiding force of our lives.

On earth as it is in heaven will also erase the very natural fear of death. We are to be so like Christ that our lives become as infinity pools where we can scarcely distinguish where earth ends and heaven begins. Indeed, our earthly life should flow effortlessly into everlasting life. For the Christian, death is but a portal to eternity.

The loss of my husband changed me forever. But on that night, I genuinely believe that Jerry did not experience death. He simply walked from this life into the next, just as though he stood in the midst of an infinity pool, realizing that earth and heaven are not separate, but unified – each a part of the other.

Jerry moved from life to life. Those of us who loved him were the ones who experienced death – the agony of his physical death and the loss of someone we deeply cherished.

When I last saw Jerry, he was at peace. Though his physical death was only moments away, he was at peace. He knew Christ and he was unafraid. Just then, I believe Jerry faced something akin to an infinity pool, a moment where earth flowed beautifully and effortlessly into heaven.

" . . . your kingdom come, your will be done on earth as it is in heaven."

Just then, standing at the threshold of infinity, I believe Jerry reached for his Savior, confidently took one step forward, and peacefully walked into eternity.

> *I want to know Christ*
> *and the power of his resurrection*
> *and the fellowship of sharing in his sufferings,*
> *becoming like him in his death,*
> *and so, somehow,*
> *to attain the resurrection of the dead.*
>
> *--Philippians 3:10-11*

A Grave, Eternal Choice

*C*old, gray, and overcast. A chilly wind drifted through the crowd, a chill I felt certain originated deep within my shattered heart. Dazed and silent, I sat beside an open grave in Birmingham, Alabama. Within minutes, my husband, Jerry, would be buried there.

Services had been held near our home in Georgia. Quite a few. Jerry was an Ordained Minister in the United Methodist Church and congregations he served celebrated his life and ministry. But for the burial we traveled to Birmingham, the place he once called home.

The scene is sealed in my mind's eye. Friends huddled beneath green tents emblazoned with the name of a local funeral home. Despite heavy coats and gloves, a tiny cloud of frost danced from their mouths when they spoke. Beneath the tent, I sat silently in a frigid metal chair, my feet resting on green Astroturf covering the wintry ground. I did not feel the cold. In fact, I did not feel anything except a sense of horror and bewilderment.

Why was I sitting in a front row seat normally reserved for widows? I was much too young for that chair. Why was I shivering in Birmingham when I wanted nothing more than to be snuggling by a fireplace with my husband? Jerry and I should have been inside our home in Georgia, laughing, reading, or talking. Our time could have been filled with a million things. But time had stopped for Jerry. It seemed to have stopped for me as well. Numbness enveloped me as I sat in

169

my front row chair and stared into the deep, black hole that, within moments, would hold the physical remains of the person I loved most in this world.

I hated that hole.

Worried friends watched me, each wanting to speak magic words that would make the hurt go away. But no such words existed. The minister read passages meant to comfort and soothe. The language was familiar but it did not reach me that day. I could only stare at the hole that would soon possess the body that was Jerry's and, with it, our broken dreams and unfulfilled future.

When the service ended, Jerry's friends stood in groups, laughing, crying, and sharing their memories of a wonderful man. I felt only an overwhelming urge to be alone . . . alone one last time with my husband. I walked to the edge of the grave and faced several black holes at that moment – one in my heart, one in my spirit, and the one dug deep into the cold ground.

The black hole in my heart burned with the hurt of profound loss, the anger of having no one to blame, and the fear of what the future held for me. Did I, in fact, have a future or would I feel this despondent for the rest of my life?

The black hole in my spirit churned as I questioned my faith in a loving God. How could God possibly love me yet allow my husband to die? Didn't God understand how desperately I needed Jerry? My husband was the only person who ever showed me unconditional love. The life we shared was genuine and wonderful. Why did it have to end so soon? Could God fathom my hurt?

The black hole in the cold ground was the most disturbing of all because it challenged precious values I had held for many years.

"Why, God? Why? Do you know how mad I am at you? Or are you even out there?"

I admitted my anger and doubt because it was naïve to think that God did not already know my feelings.

So how was it possible that, even then, I felt God's presence? I heard God speak to me and I was surprised. To be perfectly honest, I was angry and really did not feel I was on speaking terms with God at that moment. Nonetheless, I felt love enfolding me as I literally stood at the edge of my faith.

"What do you believe, Cathy?" God whispered on the wind.

"I believe Jerry is gone. I believe you could have stopped it. I'm terrified. I'm furious. I'm hurt. I'm lonely. And I don't understand."

"What else do you believe, Cathy?"

"I don't know what I believe. Do you even care? What difference does it make, God?"

"Oh, Cathy, it makes all the difference!"

I was crying, warm tears spilling from my eyes into the black hole. I was lonely, but I was not crying for Jerry. I was afraid, but I was not crying for me. The tears came because I was at a crossroad that demanded a decision.

"What do you believe, Cathy? The choice is yours. Do you believe *nothing* or do you believe *everything?* This is your moment. What is faith? You wonder if I am here? Then it is time to decide."

Dazed and overwhelmed, I felt as though I was staring into the very face of eternity. My emotions were murky and my spirit as gloomy as the wintry sky. Making even the simplest decision seemed beyond me, yet I felt God nudging me to resolve my nagging questions.

Though completely confused, I recognized that the direction of my life would be determined by the choices I made at the edge of the black hole.

"Of course I believe in you," I affirmed, reminding God of my credentials. I had attended outstanding schools and earned degrees in religion and Christian Education. My transcripts proved I studied and performed well. I had taught Sunday School, directed choirs, served at soup kitchens, and visited nursing homes. I had worked with children from the darkest corners of Atlanta as well as those from the most affluent suburban neighborhoods. I had led retreats, planned Wednesday night programs, and served on church staffs. I had married a minister! I had typed bulletins and church reports, played piano, and taught Vacation Bible School. I even baked and decorated each year as we prepared for Christmas Open House at our parsonage.

For God's sake, I was practically a *Professional Christian*!

But, God was not interested in my resume. He wanted only my complete honesty as, through my grief and anger, I determined what I believed within the deepest part of me. Did I believe God existed and loved me so totally that it cost him the life of his only son? Or did I believe all this "church stuff" was a nice fairy tale with no real truth to back it up? Was I merely working at being a Christian or was I truly seeking the face of God? Facing the blackest hole of my life, I opened my mind, heart, and soul before the God I both worshipped and questioned.

"What do you believe, Cathy?"

⧗⧗⧗⧗⧗⧗⧗

I have told you these things,
so that in me you may have peace.
In this world you will have trouble.
But take heart!
I have overcome the world.

John 16:33

I have learned a few things during my years. I know that no one makes it through life unscathed. We live in an imperfect world where trying times await each of us. Even Jesus Christ lived a life beset with trouble and pain. His heartbreaking words on the cross echoed the same emotion I felt that cold January day: "My God, My God, why have you forsaken me?" (Matthew 27:46).

Nothing.

Jesus faced his own black hole at that moment. Still, amid the horror of his death, he ultimately declared, "Father, into your hands I commit my spirit." (Luke 23:46).

Everything.

On some occasion, each of us will meet our own black hole and confront the merit of our faith. Each of us will encounter a moment when our faith is tested by events we could never have envisioned when, in blessed innocence, we spun in tire swings or built sand castles on the shore. Our lives can change dramatically in a millisecond. Experiences may overwhelm us so completely that we gasp for breath and question principles we have always believed to be true and steadfast. Without warning we may feel as lost as the iceberg that calves from the glacier into the cold sea. We struggle to upright ourselves as beliefs we once held sacred are challenged.

Maybe a diagnosis is confirmed, a fortune is lost, a marriage ends, or a child makes an unfortunate choice.

Or maybe we stand in a cemetery beside a black, gaping hole that awaits the earthly body of someone we hold dear.

Allow the words of the Son of God – a man who was despised, rejected and acquainted with sorrows – to comfort you (Isaiah 53:3).

Shortly before his own death, Jesus Christ reminded us, "In this world you will have trouble" (John 16:33). He knew this through his own experience.

Ours is an imperfect world filled with many troubles. I cannot explain why and I desperately wish things were different. But I cannot change this fact of life. I can, however, hold close to the words of assurance Jesus spoke at the end of this verse: "But take heart! I have overcome the world" (John 16:33).

Knowing Jesus Christ struggled with many of the same emotions I confront brings me great comfort. Jesus showed us the face of God. When we meet Christ, we meet God (John 14:9-11). We do not meet God by waving our list of accomplishments and good works. We meet God by loving. We meet God by trusting that Jesus Christ did overcome the world and, by doing so, opened the door to eternity for us all.

⧗⧗⧗⧗⧗⧗⧗

That cold January day is forever sealed in my mind's eye. I have now been a widow longer than I was a bride. I wish I could tell you that everything is wonderful. I wish I could say that one magic day, the hurt suddenly went away. I cannot. There are wonderful moments, of course. But there are also days when I miss Jerry so desperately that I want to stay in bed with the blankets over my head. Some days I actually do that. But I do not remain there.

Why?

Because I met God anew on a cold January day as I stood beside an open black hole. I heard his whisper. I felt his love. Still suffering the hurt and confusion of my loss, I ultimately stood tall and affirmed then and for all time, "I choose *everything*."

Making peace with this one issue has not chased away the ache and loneliness, but it has placed everything in a more appropriate perspective.

I am certain that God is love and loves even me. I am certain that Jesus Christ came to show me the face of God and to offer eternal life. I am certain that, through the Holy Spirit, God is with me in every experience of my life. I am certain that, even though I will face trouble, nothing in this life shall separate me from the love of God (Romans 8:38~39). And I am certain that in God's own time, I will see Jerry again – alive, happy, and with a perfect body.

How can I be certain of these things?

Because I chose *EVERYTHING*.

And that has made all the difference.

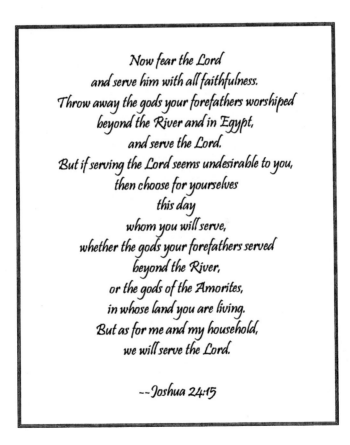

*Now fear the Lord
and serve him with all faithfulness.
Throw away the gods your forefathers worshiped
beyond the River and in Egypt,
and serve the Lord.
But if serving the Lord seems undesirable to you,
then choose for yourselves
this day
whom you will serve,
whether the gods your forefathers served
beyond the River,
or the gods of the Amorites,
in whose land you are living.
But as for me and my household,
we will serve the Lord.*

--Joshua 24:15

About the Author

Award-winning author, Cathy Lee Phillips, has written for numerous publications including *Angels on Earth, Today's Christian Woman,* and *The Sunday School Leader,* a publication of the United Methodist Publishing House. Her stories may also be found in *Don't Stop Laughing Now!* and *Look Who's Laughing!* – a series of books published by Zondervan highlighting the best in Christian humor. Cathy's regular column, *Laugh and Learn,* appears in the *Wesleyan Christian Advocate,* the Official News Source of the United Methodist Church in Georgia.

In addition to *Aging, Ailments, and Attitudes,* Cathy has authored *Silver in the Slop* and *Gutsy Little Flowers,* both of which are collections of short parables using ordinary objects and events to teach eternal truths. Her third book, *Silver Reflections: A Daily Journal,* guides readers in recognizing and appreciating the everyday blessings we so often take for granted. Printed in full color, this perpetual journal offers Scripture, quotations, and space for recording daily thoughts and observations.

While addressing serious issues, Cathy sprinkles great doses of humor throughout her writing and speaking. In fact, "humor with a message" has been called the "hallmark" of her ministry.

In addition to writing, Cathy is a popular speaker, humorist, singer, and event leader. Her unique life experiences, combined with her Master's Degree in Christian Education, enable her to weave the truth of the gospel into both the sorrows and celebrations of life.

Currently the President of Patchwork Press, Ltd., Cathy spends her days working, laughing, learning, and aging, in her home state of Georgia.

Booking Information

To schedule Cathy Lee Phillips for your event, please contact:

Stacy Robinson
The Robinson Agency
1946 Kensington High Street
Lilburn, Georgia 30047~2524
770~736~0775, Phone
770~982~8988, Fax
1~800~782~2995, Toll Free
www.TheRobinsonAgency.com

or

Patchwork Press, Ltd.
P. O. Box 4684
Canton, Georgia 30115
770~720~7988, Phone
www.patchworkpress.com

Order Books Today!

Patchwork Press, Ltd.
P. O. Box 4684
Canton, Georgia 30115
770-720-7988 - www.patchworkpress.com

Prices Effective August 1, 2003 (Prices Include Tax)

Aging, Ailments, and Attitudes: _____ copies @ $17 each = _____

Silver Reflections: A Daily Journal: _____ copies @ $17 each = _____

Gutsy Little Flowers: _____ copies @ $13 each = _____

Silver in the Slop: _____ copies @ $12 each = _____

Shipping and Handling: _____
($ 1.00 per book ordered)

Total Amount of Order: _____

· ·

Make checks payable to Patchwork Press, Ltd.,
or pay by Visa, MasterCard, or Discover.

Credit Card Number:_____
Name of Cardholder:_____
Expiration Date:_____ Signature:_____

· ·

Please Ship Books to:

Name:_____
Address:_____
City:_____ State:_____ Zip: _____
Phone:_____ E-Mail: _____